THE VILLAGE SCHOOL for Early Childhood:

Challenges for the New Millenium

By

Georgia Palmer

1st Books Library
Bloomington, Indiana
www.1stbooks.com

ISBN: 0-75963-946-9

This book is printed on acid free paper.

Book Cover designed
by Susan Hargraves

1stBooks – rev. 06/20/01

Your children are not your children.
They are the sons and daughters of Life's longing for itself.
They come through you but not from you,
And though they are with you they belong not to you.
You may give them your love but not your thoughts,
For they have their own thoughts.
You may house their bodies but not their souls,
For their souls dwell in the house of tomorrow,
Which you cannot visit, not even in your dreams.
You may strive to be like them, but seek not to make them like you
For life goes not backward nor tarries with yesterday.
You are the bows from which your children as living arrows are sent forth.
The archer sees the mark upon the path of the infinite
And he bends you with his might that his arrows may go swift and far.
Let your bending in the archer's hand be for gladness'
For even as he loves the arrow that flies,
So he loves the bow that is stable.

---Kahlil Gibran

For
my beloved family
Joe, Anne, Susan, Jason
Wayne, Rob
Ed and Kathrin

Thanks to my good teachers and mentors
Who inspired me and taught me well:

Muriel Farrell
Rosalyn Shen
Claudia Lewis
Bettison Shapiro
Lane Weidmann
Leah Levinger
Alverta McKenzie

TABLE OF CONTENTS

CHAPTER 1 LOOKING TOWARD THE FUTURE

The new century and new millenium brings with it dreams of a brighter, better future. Long cherished hopes stir anew in our hearts for a chance to reinvent and to expand existing structures and to improve them. There is an urge to "clean house," to throw out all the old tired, worn out ways of thinking and feeling and doing and replacing them with new ways which are more relevant to the times we live in. Many of the old paradigms no longer apply. The world is changing so quickly around us that many of us have not noticed the need to adjust our perceptions to a new reality. The old stereotype of the idyllic mother-homemaker baking cookies and spending all her time and energy raising and nurturing her children is a thing of the past. The overwhelming majority of mothers today are in the workplace, either out of necessity or out of choice. Whether we like it or not, this is the reality. It is not likely that this trend will reverse itself in the years to come. The role of mothers will never become obsolete, of course. Parents will, in spite of their conflicting roles and responsibilities, always remain the the main source of love and strength for their growing children. But, they will need more help and better help than they have ever needed before. There is and will continue to be an ever increasing need for good quality early education. Early education has been given many names—preschool, nursery school, kindergarten, Head Start, day care. Regardless of what they are called, they have the same goal in common, the goal of educating young children to become the best they can be, for their sake and for the sake of the coming generation of citizens. Early childhood educators must be prepared. We must decide what characteristics we want to develop in our young children in order to build the kind of society we aspire to. We must begin to plan ahead to meet this urgent need head on. We will need more programs and we will need to improve the programs we have. Many new competent teachers will need to be trained. In order to attract these good teachers, they must be given the recognition, respect and status they richly deserve. They also must be paid a salary in accordance with the standards of all other teachers. Good early education must become available to all young children, whether their parents can afford it or not. Young children whose mothers cannot be home are our most vulnerable young children. Public education must be provided for them which is committed to sound practices. If the law requires welfare mothers to seek employment, then we must provide the best possible education and care for their children. The idea that good day care should be available to all with or without cost is revolutionary, just as the idea of free kindergarten once was. But, it's time is coming.

THE VILLAGE SCHOOL

The familiar African saying that "it takes a village to raise a child" is so true. Love, security and self-esteem come initially and primarily from the home. Yet, the larger society must also take responsibility for every child in it if it wants to be functional and healthy. Parents need the assistance of the "village" to provide a good support system. They are all our children. Their welfare is for the good of us all in the long run. Good care and good education for all children will create a stronger, safer, brighter future for all of us.

In this new vision of the future the old names of early childhood programs may no longer be appropriate. "Preschool" implies that it is a place for children to be prior to "real school," as though the learning that takes place there is not "real" learning. Kindergarten, too often, is seen as only having the function of reading readiness for first grade. Three year olds and 4's and 5's have their own educational needs determined by their own level of understanding and perception. They can learn from every experience they are exposed to. The next level will take care of itself as they develop and mature. Head Start is a good name and a good program, though limited to the economically disadvantaged, it comes the closest to the Village School ideal. The Montessori Schools are also good models of early education. The term "Day Care" seems to imply custodial care only, a place to park children to keep them physically safe until their parents return. A new all inclusive term needs to be coined to cover all schools for young children. They are schools in every sense of the word. Just because they teach younger children does not make them less so. A good name to cover our ideal early childhood programs of the future might be Village Schools. The school represents the "village" of our own community, becomes the extention of the family, raising the children together in accordance with the values, standards, beliefs, customs and skills of our society.

THE PARENT CENTER

The Village School will also be a center for parents to hone their parenting skills. Classes in child development and creative parenting will be offered. Each school will include a parent community room for seminars, discussions and speakers. Each school will include on the staff a counselor who will coordinate these activities, be available for conferences with individual parents to discuss specific day-to-day problems in raising children, to give suggestions and advice. The counselor will be familiar with other community resources and be able to make referrals for more serious problems. Parent-teacher conferences will be held in the parent room. Literature and articles on the subject of parenting will be displayed here. It will be a place where parents will be able to socialize with other parents and share their experiences over a cup of coffee. A small kitchen with a stove, sink, refrigerator and coffee maker will be included in this area. This arrangement would solidify the community, give moral support to busy parents, educate them in the best ways to provide a positive home atmosphere for their children and help them to understand the significance of a good education. The Village School and the parents will become partners in the important task of raising children. It would include parents to a larger degree in their children's school lives during those hours when they cannot be with them.

WEEDING OUT THE BAD PROGRAMS

There are many outstanding early childhood schools in existence today. The Village School will take the best features from their model and use them in their plans. In planning Village Schools these good programs will be analyzed and utilized. They will constitute the blueprint that will be followed. There also exist many, many low quality programs. These have exploded out of the urgent need for some kind of child care for working mothers. Since there is a desperate shortage of any kind of day care, mothers must choose from the limited list that is available. They must also find one they can afford, since it is not usually free. The need is sometimes so immediate that mothers don't have enough time to research them thoroughly enough before they decide to entrust their children to them. Their main concern is to find a place that will be safe and that their children will be returned to them at the end of the day in the same condition in which they left them. Often in their desperation, mothers will hand their children over to the lady down the street who wants added income. The worst of the day care centers have been known to abuse children. Most of them are safe enough and fulfill their roles as custodial caretakers well enough. Custodial care demands little skill or insight. It does not require much in the way of equipment, materials or supplies. They often operate on a shoestring and the little they can afford is minimal. They do not think of themselves as schools and they do not teach formally. However, young children learn from everything and they learn all the time. In an impoverished setting they will learn the wrong things. They will learn passivity. They will learn that it is not acceptable to be curious, to explore, to question because it will be inconvenient for the adults to whom neatness and order and convenience are high priorities. They will learn that conformity is the greatest virtue. The danger is that they will learn not to trust adults and not to trust themselves. In order to avoid having to meet the standards that state departments of education require of schools for staff, equipment, space and program, these day care facilities insist that they are "not teaching anything" and therefore not subject to scrutiny. The job of supervising them falls to the Department of Health and Welfare because they are not considered schools. This status simply gives them permission to be bad schools. Every day care center, planned or unplanned, good or bad, is a school. We must get rid of the bad ones and replace them with good ones.

Another form of less-than-top quality program is the Play School. These often identify themselves as nursery schools and are well-meaning. They would not think of having a television set and they look down on custodial day care. They spend much of their available funds on elaborate playground equipment like merry-go-rounds and swings. These are more amusements than they are tools for learning. They contain their own brand of passivity. Their passivity stems from inadequate goals. They stress socialization and fun above all other goals. Their main aim is a kindly one: for the children to be happy. They give the children great freedom to play, play, play. They are let loose and intervention by the teacher happens only if there is an accident or a quarrel. They are not guided toward experiences that will enhance their learning about the world they live in. Play and joy are a worthy and necessary part of early childhood education, but the educational challege is to bring joy through maximum learning. The teacher is not just a play supervisor, but a skilled leader who is sensitive to the potentiality for sound learning experiences. She knows what children are doing and what they are learning as they play. She opens up new choices and challenges for them, all unobtrusively. The Village School will integrate the play and the fun and joy into its program but extend it to include more constructive learning.

Then there are the "Pushy Programs." The overriding goal of these programs is to get the children ready for the first grade, first grade being the standard-bearer of all things desirable. Parents often create a climate to which these schools cater. These parents are sure their children are smarter, more developed, more sophisticated than average and that they should not be held back doing "childish" things. They want to give them a head start on reading. They think they are preparing them for future success. They are already planning what college they will go to. Teachers begin to feel the pressure. They forget to plan for these young children's present needs. These "get-them-ready-for-first-grade" kindergartens equate this readiness with conformity. Their aim is to produce a child who will fit in and not cause any trouble. This attitude erases individuality and self-expression and dampens real motivation for learning. They are given drab, artificial paper and pencil exercises which is supposed to accelerate "reading readiness." They forget that readiness is internal and set by nature. Good kindergartens and first grades teach reading to those children who are ready in lively functional ways which are in harmony with their individual maturity level. Good first grade teachers will have their own goals and plans for teaching and good kindergartens have their own legitimate agenda. The Village School will not be pushy. It will have a program that is appropriate for the level of the children it serves.

CHAPTER 2 BASIC PROPOSITIONS AND PHILOSOPHY

BASIC GUIDELINES FOR THE VILLAGE SCHOOL

Children's early childhood years are critical for what they learn and will continue to learn and for the people they will ultimately become. The way in which professional communities move forward in developing education programs for young children is more crucial than ever today, especially in view of the increasing numbers of one parent homes and the exodus of mothers out of the home and into the work place. New welfare laws make it mandatory for young mothers to seek employment within a specified time. There is a need, reaching almost crisis proportions, for good professionally planned preschools and day care facilities to emerge to fill the gap. Good early childhood care and education must become an extention of the home and provide some of the elements that were formerly the sole responsibility of the parents. This realistic fact opens great possibilities for educators, but also charges them with tremendous responsibilities. Within these parameters lies the possibility for creating a firm foundation for learning and healthy growth. There also exists the possibility of hazards to the growth and development of these vulnerable young children. All depends upon the integrity, knowledge and concern of the those to whom these children are entrusted.

PURPOSES

Planners of a good educational program for infants and toddlers and children between the ages of three and six must have a clear concept of what the needs of these young children are and what the purpose of their education encompasses. They must be sure that their programs are based on a heart-felt philosophy of education. A good program must include a statement of basic assumptions and knowledge. It must carefully and thoughtfully establish guidelines for an effective program based on that philosophy and knowledge. It must be understood by all from the beginning that school is not a baby-sitting service in which children are handed over temporarily with the sole purpose of keeping them physically safe until the parent is free to resume their care. The school is entrusted with the important function of the personality development of human beings, of their social and intellectual growth. It must be understood that these young human beings need certain early childhood experiences before they can take advantage of later experiences.

The purpose of school is learning. But, it must be remembered that children of different ages learn in different ways. Because some parents are so concerned with giving their little ones a "head start," by preparing them too early for the academics to come, some pre-schools acquiesce to the parents wishes and anxieties by pushing reading too early. They think that they are preparing them for future academic success. This is equivalent to picking fruit off the tree before it is ripe. It will never reach the same potential for sweetness and taste that it might have had it been picked at its peak of readiness. There is a wide-spread assumption abroad that children of early years and their teachers are of minor consequence intellectually and that the sooner we get on with their "real" education the better. This assumption does not allow for the fact that there exists a developmental sequence through which all children pass. Certain concepts cannot be fully understood before some degree of maturing takes place. The exact time of this maturing varies with individual children and is not necessarily correlated with intelligence. A child will not miss the boat if his learning to read is postponed until later. But, teaching him to read before he is ready can be harmful to his development by making him feel frustrated and inadequate. It is more vital for young children to experience their own fullness of being through sensory experiences which lead to competence and confidence in their bodies and minds, than to pursue abstract symbolism too soon. Seeds grow with the help of an internal timeclock provided by the life force of nature. Given good soil, water and sunlight and they will grow at their own rate. No amount of prodding will make them grow any faster. We must have faith that they will grow and blossom in their own time. So it is with young children. We can provide the best atmosphere and climate and care and have faith that they will grow and learn.

A child needs to follow a pattern of growth natural for him in order to realize his fullest potential as a person. Many young children have experienced such disrupted and disordered lives that they cannot make the most use of learning situations until they can compensate for certain gaps in their development. Some come from homes that are so precarious that they have grown to distrust adults. They have developed emotional problems due to home inconsistencies and poor family relationships. A good educational program can fill some of those gaps. Such children can find some measure of stability, security, basic trust, support, encouragement and a sense of identity, so necessary to further growth toward social and intellectual learning. What is most important for all children during these early years is to experience a quality of living that provides for growth that is continuous and interrelated and relevant to their current stage of development.

PHILOSOPHY OF EDUCATION

A philosophy of education must be more than words. It must encompass beliefs about the nature of early childhood development that come directly from the heart. The curriculum, the facilities, the social climate, the goals and the objectives, the teaching staff, the materials and tools provided must be an outgrowth of this philosophy. These beliefs will create the desired atmosphere. Each individual educator will have his own belief and philosophy depending on his own perspective. This is mine:

I believe that the preservation of human dignity is of primary and monumental importance in the development of the human personality. All else follows: self-confidence, self-respect, independence, self-control, self-mastery and respect for others. The teacher provides and develops an atmosphere of mutual respect, justice, positive values, friendly understanding, warmth and love. If a child is liked and respected for himself, he will like and respect himself enough to like and respect others. Then his energies can be directed toward the constructive and purposeful task of learning.

I believe that children should be allowed to do their own learning. Intellectual development proceeds at its own pace. The teacher's role is to present situations in which constructive experience becomes possible. The child himself experiments, explores, manipulates, seeks answers, makes discoveries.

The teacher sets the stage, provides the best creative materials, encourages and and reinforces learning, nurtures an intellectually stimulating atmosphere which is conducive to learning and growth.

CURRICULUM

The Village School provides opportunities for children to experience their world by experiencing themselves in relationship to it. If the climate is favorable and safe, they will unfold in confidence and security toward a greater independence, spontaneity, creativity and self-discipline. They will find pleasure and satisfaction in learning and in communicating and living with others. The curriculum is primarily concerned with social living, creative expression, and physical and intellectual growth.

SOCIAL LIVING

Out of their experience in social living, children will gain a stronger sense of identity. The questions "Who am I?" and "What can I do?" will be explored. They will learn that they have an identity and a personality of their own apart from their families. They will learn that they can be happy and safe in another place away from home. They will gain a sense of belonging. "I am a successful member of a group. I like others and others like me." They will learn what is acceptable behavior in a group from the climate of the classroom and from their peers. They will develop a sense of justice. "What is fair?" "Who can I trust?" "Why must I share?" They will learn that responsibility and self-control are directly correlated with group harmony and group membership. They will learn about their own and other's feelings and how to deal with those feelings.

CREATIVITY

In a good school atmosphere children will be able to explore their own creative inclinations. They will learn to represent their own ideas in their own way. They will learn to think freely and to gain confidence in their own ability to originate. They will learn constructive, thoughtful and concentrated use of tools and materials. Learning that things have proper places will free them from the distractions of disorder so that they can make the best use of their creative and intellectual powers. They will learn that accomplishment, pride and pleasure are the rewards of creative effort.

INTELLECTUAL GROWTH

Intellectual growth is an important goal in a good curriculum. Scientific Method is a part of experience in all areas of activity, indoors and outdoors. The children are learning to question, to wonder, to seek answers, to investigate, to experiment, to experience the joy of discovery. They must be provided with ample time to explore and to digest what is learned and experienced. The teacher's role is to clarify, broaden and extend their concepts. She helps them to organize their thoughts and to create order in their minds. She encourages them to solve their problems and to think for themselves. She sets a good model for them to follow by her patience and her sense of timing and justice. She listens. She inspires them with her own enthusiasm and her own attitude toward learning.

PHYSICAL GROWTH

It is important to provide adequate space for outdoor play. Young children need the opportunity to develop their large muscles and to use their own bodies to discover and explore mass, weight, substance, relativity and the motion of the world around them in relation to themselves. They need to climb on top of, into, outside of large objects and feel them with their own senses. They need to slide and swing and roll in order to feel the rhythms and movements in the earth for themselves. They need to expend their energies in constructive ways that are conducive to their healthful physical growth.

THE TEACHER'S ROLE

The key to a good program is an effective teacher. She or he must have professional qualifications and a broad, liberal education. The teacher must have studied child development, early childhood education including its history and philosophy, the behavioral and social sciences, early childhood and elementary curriculum, and student teaching under the supervision of a qualified supervisor. This is the minimal prerequisite for being placed in a position of responsibility for the education of young children. Teaching an early childhood program is an art that requires a special quality of personality. It is not for everyone. It requires a special patience, flexibility, inner stability, clarity of purpose, a thoughtful mind, empathy for and a belief in people, and a questioning and innovative spirit. The teacher must be able to establish and develop warm relationships and be able to communicate significantly with children and with parents. She must not be afraid of feelings or the open expression of them. She must be spontaneous and real. Small children can sense immediately if adults are genuine in their interactions with them.

A good teacher must understand how children learn and be sensitive to their individual state of readiness and their individual interests. She must be flexible enough in her approach to appreciate the principle of integrative teaching. As young children learn, they integrate their various experiences into an integrative whole, each on his own, through play. Whatever they observe and assimilate comes together into a concept and an understanding of their world.

The good teacher must develop a style of communication that is non-authoritarian and still retain the authority of an adult worthy of respect without abusing her position. Her authority must be established on genuine and authentic justice and trust. She must be capable of responding to immature behavior with a mature attitude by not taking personally the childrens' expression of hostility. Rather she must devise ways to teach them more constructive methods of dealing with their feelings. She will show them by her actions that, although she may not approve of what they do, she still likes and respects them. She will channel their behavior constructively. She will let it be known that she is there to protect everyone in the group equally and will not allow anyone to be harmed or interfered with. She will make each child understand that she will stop him from behaving in a way that is destructive to himself or others until he is ready to stop himself. Her ultimate goal is teaching self-discipline. She must also be able to differentiate between the children's emotional needs and her own. It is very important that she does not exaggerate their expressions of admiration for her in order to fulfill her own emotional needs.

THE ASSISTANT TEACHER

The role of the assistant teacher is invalluble. She or he lends much needed support to the group teacher and to the program. She is there ready to step in whenever the teacher needs backup. When the teacher is dealing individually with a child who is having a problem, the assistant teacher fills in, helping to keep the pace and keeping the program flowing smoothly. She takes her cues from the group teacher and instinctively follows through with the goals of the day. She helps with the physical demands of the program, such as helping the children dress and undress, setting out materials, cleaning up after a messy project. She develops an ear for the harmony or disharmony of the room and steps in at the appropriate moment to restore stability to the atmosphere in concert with the group teacher. She also develops a comfortable relationship with the children and gains their trust. Student teachers or student nurses also can be valuable and helpful as they learn.

THE ADMINISTRATION

The administration is responsible for seeing to it that the propositions and guidelines are implemented and adhered to. The administrator hires teachers and assistants who would be assets to an effective and comprehensive program and is responsible for a supportable teacher-pupil ratio. She or he works within the allotted budget to provide the best materials and equipment possible and plans the most effective use of space. The administrator must be a diplomatic liaison between the teacher and the parents.

References

Law, Norma; Moffitt, Mary; Moore, Elenora; Overfield, Ruth; Starks, Esther; Basic Propositions for Early Childhood Education. Washington, D.C. Association for Childhood Education International, 1966

CHAPTER 3 PATTERNS OF DEVELOPMENT

Children develop and grow in stages. Each stage of development is accompanied by a typical pattern of behavior and characteristics which are not necessarily an expression of the child's own basic personality. Each phase brings certain changes in physical characteristics, behavior, attitude and perceptions. There is a gradual broadening of motor, language and social abilities. These phases are common to all children in our culture.

Of course, every child will not change overnight on his birthday. There will be variations of intensity based upon the child's individual personality, experience and background. The "typical child" does not actually exist in the sense that all of the following characteristics are embodied in him at exactly the ages given. The typical child is a construct, a device used in analysis for purposes of clarification. This construct gives us a clue as to what to look for and what to expect of children at a certain level of development.

THE TYPICAL THREE-YEAR-OLD

At the age of three, a child stands on the threshold of a new kind of development. The next three years will be as important for his perceptual and emotional growth as the preceding three years had been for his physical growth and motor development. This is not to say that there has been no perceptual or motor development until the age of three or that physical and motor development will not continue. However, the rate of physical growth does slow down between the ages of three and five. The child's main purpose now is to learn through his body about his world and to develop and practice the important functions of his society. By three he has progressed from a state of complete helplessness and passivity to an ambulatory and communicative state. His body has changed in size and proportion. He has gained control of many of his muscles. At birth he weighed about seven and a half pounds and measured about twenty inches. At three he stands about thirty-eight inches high or so and weighs about thirty-five pounds. As a neonate his head was 25% of his total body length and his legs were less than 5% of him. Now his head is about 18%

of his body length and his legs are about 20% of him. He can walk even on tiptoe and run. He can jump up and down and over a short distance. He can walk upstairs alternating his feet, but not downstairs, and he can ride a tricycle. He is attempting to do some climbing but he is not too skillful at it yet. He cannot as yet throw or catch a ball. He can put on his own shoes and feed himself without too much spilling. He has control over his bladder and sphincter muscles but he may have occasional accidents when he is emotionally stimulated. At three he has about 900 words in his oral vocabulary and can recognize many more. He speaks in 2-4 word sentences. He enjoys playing with sounds, rolling them around in his mouth or throat and repeating nonsense rhymes, rhythmic syllables and chants. He repeats sounds and words in his speech (which may sound like stuttering but which is not considered as such at this age,) though not with the compulsion that he did at two. His voice is fairly well controlled, his vowels and consonents are clear. and his pronunciation of words is fairly stable. His perceptions of the world have progressed. At birth he had a vague undifferentiated perception of his environment but could not see himself as separate from it. Gradually his perceptions became more sharply defined. He could see himself as separate from his surroundings yet as someone who had a place in the environment. At three, he has some limited concepts of time, space and relationships. His perception of time is fairly limited to the immediate present.and only as it affects the performance of his daily functions. He may (or may not) be able to count to ten by rote but has little concept of numbers in groups beyond two or three. His spatial concepts are also limited to his immediate environment. He understands down, up, around, beneath, inside or on top of but he has no concept of distance. He is beginning to be aware of family stucture. He knows that mommy and daddy and baby belong to each other, but he does not understand other relationships. He might see his teacher's husband and ask if he is her daddy. He cannot distinguish between reality and fantasy; he believes dreams are real. He has not yet learned to play in groups or with another child. He plays next to another child but his activities are still his own. Three-year-olds talk at each other rather than to each other and their themes are short and disjointed. The three-year-old paints with usually only one color, testing the consistency of the paint, smearing with little thought of content, enjoying the textures rather than the form. He pounds clay for the sensory pleasure of it. He enjoys dramatic play around domestic scenes and is not concerned with sex or age in relation to the role he plays. Quarrels between three-year-olds tend to take the form of either silent tugs of war over toys or loud crying. Three-year-olds conform easily and respond to directions. They have a vague sense of right and wrong based on their parents' and teachers' expectations, but they have not internalized a conscience as such. Their fears at three are mainly visual; they are afraid of unusual looking people, masks and the "bogeyman." They are afraid of the dark, of animals, of policemen and burglers. The three-year-old cries when his mother or father go out at night. His fears show that his perceptual growth has progressed to the point where he is able to recognize danger in a situation. At each stage of development he will have new types of fears which, given guidance and understanding, he will learn to conquer. Over-all, the three-year old is in good equilibrium. He is in harmony with the people and things around him. He likes to share and is cooperative and easy going. He has in a sense reached the crest of a mountain of growth and he can now rest on his laurels. He feels secure and is now gathering strength for the next spurt of growth. During this period he is a delight to the adults around him. However, this period does not last long. By the time he is three-and-a-half he enters a new, though temporary stage of insecurity. His motor coordination may go through a period of extreme disequilibrium. He needs to reorganize his physical self into a new phase of integration before he reaches a new plateau at age five. He expresses his insecurity in whining, thumbsucking and demanding attention. At three-and-a-half a child needs a great deal of love and patience to get him safely through to the next stage.

THE TYPICAL FOUR-YEAR-OLD

The four-year-old is out of bounds emotionally and motorwise. He kicks. He hits. He throws stones. He breaks things and runs away. He indulges in loud silly laughter. Then with very little provocation he goes into a fit of rage. He is defiant and boastful. He plays "tough." This is the age when he creates imaginary companions and really believes in them. Reality and fantasy are intertwined in his mind. His time and space concepts have developed slightly since three: he has some idea of a past (he is curious about himself as a baby) and a future (he is going to marry Mommy.) He still cannot tell time and his concept of distance might have extended itself to grandma's house. His vocabulary has increased to about 1500 words and his sentences are longer by one or two words. His rate of speech is quite rapid and the volume of his voice is loud. His motor skills have improved. He can now climb well and ride a tricycle recklessly. He is beginning to learn ball throwing. though he doesn't have much control yet and can't catch. He can walk downstairs now alternating his feet. His physical growth has not increased greatly. He has gained about 5-7 pounds and grown a few inches. He is still more interested in parallel play than in group games but he is more involved in other childrens' play than he was at three. His quarrels are more frequent and involve more physical fighting. His fears are predominantly auditory: fire engines, dogs barking, storms and animals. He is afraid of the dark and of his mother's leaving at night. However, he appears, at least on the surface, to be brash and overly confident. The pendulum has swung from three-and-a half year old insecurity to the other extreme. Slowly its swing subsides after the four-year-old has had an opportunity to test himself out and run to the limits and a little beyond. Then, at four-and-a-half he begins to settle down again. He accepts limits more readily. He is making a real effort to distinguish reality from fantasy, though he is not always sure. His play is less wild, though he is still unpredictable. His coordination and motor skills are greatly improved. His concentration is more sustained. At this stage the slow talker or physically awkward child has a chance to catch up with his peers.

THE TYPICAL FIVE-YEAR-OLD

Now our typical child of five is ready to enter kindergarten. Once again he has reached a plateau in his growth and can relax to catch his breath. He has made great strides in his motor coordination. At five he has mastered the problem of asymmetry which has until now kept him carrying objects in two hands. He can swing his arms in alternating movements with his feet as he walks and can ride a tricycle with alternate and rhythmical movement. He may be able to skip. His body is beginning to lose its baby cherubic look. His head is about the size it will be when he is an adult. His legs are now 44% of his height. He has a vocabulary of over 2,000 words. His voice is well modulated and he no longer repeats words or sounds. His use of language is fairly sophisticated and reflects much humor. His perceptions have developed enough to be able to make fine distinctions between characteristics of objects and he has developed many new concepts. He can recognize and name the primary colors and usually the secondary colors as well. He knows his age, his address, and perhaps even his telephone number. He knows the numbers of his favorite TV channels. He may be able to print the letters of his first name. He can recognize and distinguish coin money, though he doesn't always understand their relative values. He is ready for the concept of number sets from 0-5. He is beginning to develop some concept of time in relation to the cycles of the seasons of the year. He understands tomorrow and yesterday, though these terms may represent to him the whole future and the whole past. He can now sit and listen to a whole story from beginning to end. His paintings show some form and control and he uses several colors. He can participate in group games and group activities. He is learning the meaning of cooperation. He is learning that he must take responsibility for his own actions and to accept the consequences of his behavior. The quality of his conscience will depend on his parents, especially to the extent that he identifies with the parent of the same sex. He is becoming self-aware. He knows what he can do, how he feels and how others respond to him. He is beginning to develop leadership qualities at this age. He is interested in everything and explores everything.. He is friendly, warm and lovable.

References

Ilg, Frances L; Ames, Louise Bates. Child Behavior. New York: Dell Publishing Company, Inc., 1955.

Spock, Dr. Benjamin. Baby and Child Care NewYork: Affiliated Publishers, 1957.

Lane, Howard; Beauchamp, Mary. Understanding Human Behavior. Englewood Cliffs, NJ: Prentice Hall, Inc. 1959.

Thompson, George. Child Psychology. Boston, Mass.: Houghton Mifflin Co., 1962.

CHAPTER 4 TRANSITION AND ADJUSTMENT

The quality of the adjustment that children first experience in a social setting apart from their families can set the tone for their entire school career. They are faced with the prospect of being physically separated from the one or two people who have until then provided all their needs and comforts. They miss the comfort of their mothers' bodies near them. In every direction away from her looms the threatening unknown. They are unconsciously afraid that new things will be expected of them that they will not be able to cope with. This anxiety is experienced by the parents as well as the children. The mother may be parted from her child for the first time since his birth. Since then she alone has been responsible for attending to his every need. Now for the first time her child will be part of a social structure in which she will have little or no part. She cannot directly control those forces in the classroom that will affect him. She wonders anxiously if he will be treated with kindness and respect for his person if she is not there to protect him. She looks for assurance that he will be understood and that his faults will be tolerated.. She is uncertain about whether he will be able to fend for himself and whether he will feel safe and secure. She wonders how he will get along with his peers in a group situation.

It is the teacher's responsibility to plan, to prepare, and to deal with this situation in such a way as to minimize and ameliorate these anxieties of both the parents and the children as quickly as possible. She must tread lightly and easily. She must create and present an atmosphere in which both parent and child will be reassured. She must inspire trust. She must project confidence, poise and gentle patience. She must be sensitive to the unspoken needs of both and to be ready to respond to those needs at the proper psychological moment.

She can begin to pave the way for that time even before the opening of school. For example, two weeks before the school year begins, she can call each set of parents for an appointment to visit each family at home. It helps to see the child, the mother, and the father if he is available, in their natural surroundings. Much can be learned about the emotional climate of the home and the relationship of the parent and child, of the mother and father to each other, and of the child and his siblings. The child gains a sense of security from having seen his teachers on his own home ground. The mother also has an opportunity to meet and speak with those who will be responsible for her child's welfare and to take their measure. The group teacher and the assistant teacher will both attend this important meeting. Each group teacher might have her own way of approaching the interview, depending on what she senses is appropriate in a given situation. An informal chat with smiles and coffee is a good ice breaker. Then a questionaire can be introduced. It might help to focus on the purpose of the visit and head off rambling into irrelevent areas. It also reveals to the mother the depth of the teacher's interest in her child. There is so much that the mother wants to tell her about him: his needs, his problems, his weaknesses, his strengths.

She wants the teacher to appreciate her child as she does and to understand him. Yet, it is difficult for her to begin. She doesn't want to appear overly concerned. Pencil poised, the teacher can begin by turning to the child and speak gently and cheerfully to him as if they are about to play a fun game. "I am going to ask you some questions and your Mommy some questions so I can find out what you like and what you don't like. Maybe Mommy will ask some questions about school. If you have any questions to ask then you ask, too. OK?" Usually the child responds very well to this. He is glad to be included as a full fledged member of the discussion. He feels important. When he is satisfied that he has had his full share of attention, the teacher is able to discuss him with his mother without subjecting him to the indignity of talking over his head. He also needs to take the teacher's measure in his own way; he is more interested in her tone, her body language, her general attitude toward him than he is in her words. Request in advance that siblings be engaged elsewhere so that he does not have to share the time with them. Speak to him and ask him questions only as long as he seems interested and responsive. If he is very shy or restless do not focus attention on him but smile warmly and allow him to sit close to his mother or to play with his toys nearby. Although he is not directly participating in the discussion, he is aware of the teacher's attitude and he is learning about her and whether he can trust her. When the mother and the teacher are talking about him, the assistant teacher can distract him with conversation, a book, or a visit to his room to see his favorite toys. The teacher can then ask the mother brief questions about the child's health, the family structure, and about his routines and habits. Allow the most time for the last three questions.1) What do you like most about your child? 2) What has been your greatest problem with him? 3) How do you expect him to adjust to separation from you? The answers may take many forms and go in different directions depending on the mother's own personality and style of communication. Leave it open. Listen and learn from her tone, body language and words. Write down as much as is possible. The questionaire has served it's purpose. It has given the mother a chance to say all that is on her mind in the shortest time possible and she is assured that the teacher has been listening.

It is best to keep the group small the first day of school. Half the group can come in on Thursday and the other half on Friday. (They will then have the weekend to spend with their families.) That way individual attention can be given to each child. He is better able to acclimate himself to the room if there are fewer children present using the equipment, moving around, making sounds, perhaps crying. When the group is small he is less likely to be overwhelmed and more likely to get friendly with the other children. He leaves with a feeling of success. The first day is half the length in time. This puts less strain on the child. The schedule is the same but each period is shorter. He becomes familiar with the routine and with the climate of the classroom and before he has a chance to get too anxious it is time to go home.

Mothers or fathers should be encouraged to stay with their children for the first few days. Coffee can be served in a meeting room or in the hall with seats provided. As each child appears to be ready, parents can try to leave the room, but be available outside the room. It may be important for the child to know that if he needs his mother she will appear even though she may now be out of sight. Thus he learns that comfort and security are possible to attain quickly even if he doesn't see his mother every minute of the day. There may be frequent trips outside the door to see if she is still there, for those children who need assurance. Being allowed to observe the classroom for a few days is also important in alleviating some of the mother's anxiety. She learns what will be expected of her child.and she will be able to assess his ability to adjust. She gets a mental picture of the routines, the activities, the climate of the classroom and the personality of the teacher. If she is comforted and she relaxes, the child is likely to make his adjustment sooner. Her attitude will be transmitted to him with or without words.

Under this system of preparation, it usually follows that after the third day the majority of the children in the group are ready to participate with a minimum of anxiety.There is a group dynamic at work here. As the anxious child sees the other mothers leaving, he too wants to aspire toward independence and he strives toward what he senses to be the group norm. He observes also the manner in which the ones who cry are comforted and he knows that he too will be comforted by the teacher if he needs it. There are usually about four or five children who display no anxiety. These are children who are accustomed to being with people other than their mothers for some part of the day or who have a high proportion of confidence and basic trust. They usually settle into the routine easily and enjoy the variety of materials and toys and the company of the other children. The home visit, the familiarity with the teacher, the assurance that the mother will come if needed is enough to satisfy them. They set the norm for the others. The mothers of these children are usually positive and relaxed people. Often they do not feel the need to stay after the first day. They might bring the child in on the second day and say, "He'll be all right!" and leave with a confident goodbye. By the end of the first week, there will usually be only about two or three mothers left who remain somewhere in the building. One of these may still be unable to leave the room even for short periods without the child crying. By the end of the second week, it can be expected that all children will be able to stay without their mothers. There are exceptions. Some may have to stay as long as four weeks, but that would be an unusually insecure child or possibly an unusually insecure mother. In such a case it is often the mother who cannot separate from her child. After this initial period of adjustment, there may be regressions when some problem triggers off an anxious reaction. By then, however, the teacher and child have developed a close enough relationship for him to accept comfort from her. If his anxiety is severe, his mother can be called to come. Sometimes it is enough just to have him speak to her on the phone.

After the children have been in school for one month or more, it is time to have a meeting with the parents during which school methods, goals and philosophy are reiterated. The teacher will stress again that she is approachable, that she wishes to work with them and that she welcomes their interest and suggestions. It may be the first opportunity for the fathers to meet the teachers. Following the meeting, parents and teachers can meet individually and informally. It is a meeting that marks the end of the adjustment period. The mothers are usually all smiles and they express their delight and surprise at the quick way their children adjusted and at the degree of pleasure with which they come to school. "She loves it!" "She cries when it is Saturday or Sunday and she can't come to school!" " I thought Johnny would never let me leave without crying. I was ready to give up. Now he loves to come." The teacher knows that she has succeeded and it feels good.

From that time on the child's energies can be directed into constructive learning. The process has already begun. He has learned the most basic and vital of lesson in social living. He has learned it not only on the intellectual and conscious level, but on the vital level which is at the core of his being. He has made his first major adjustment. He will carry it into every aspect of his life for a long time to come.

SEPARATION ANXIETY

These are some examples of how different children and mothers behaved while experiencing separation anxiety and how the anxiety was alleviated.

Katy's case is an illustration of the fact that even if it is impossible for the mother to stay until her child is completely ready to let her go, it usually works out anyway.

KATY

Katy's parents had been separated since Katy was five months old. The separation was an amicable one and they were cooperative in the raising of their two children. Although the older brother had great difficulty adjusting to the subsequent divorce, Katy never seemed to suffer much as a result of it. She adored her father and saw him frequently. The mother was a social worker. The first three days of school she took off from her job to be with Katy. However, she could not stay beyond that time and so, even though Katy cried and clung to her mother every morning, she had to hand her over to me and leave. I felt that in Katy's case this would not cause any major trauma; she seemed stable enough to weather it. Katy would be pried from her mother's arms and neck gently. The mother would hand her over to me and leave no matter how much Katy cried. She cried for perhaps ten to twenty minutes every morning for about five days. I would hold her very close and rock her gently. I would say, "You want your mother, I know. I understand that you want your Mommy. Stay here with me until you feel better." I did not try to amuse her or distract her but accepted her feeling. Katy snuggled up and relaxed and soon stopped crying. After a while she scrambled down and started to play. On the sixth day she no longer cried. On the seventh day, she walked in with a big smile and announced happily, "I'm here!"

The following example of Clifford is the severest case of separation anxiety of a mother that I have ever observed. It is not typical:

CLIFFORD

Clifford's mother was the problem. She was older than most mothers of three-year-olds. He had been like a gift from heaven long after she had given up hope of ever having a child. The father was a clinical psychologist and she had worked as a school psychologist. They had agreed that they would use their knowledge of human behavior to raise a perfect child who would not suffer the usual emotional conflicts. He would grow, she thought, like a flower in the sun of their devotion and unlimited love. Consequently, Clifford reached the age of three without ever knowing the frustrations that result from living in a social world nor did he experience any limitations to his behavior. His mother paved the way for him and supervised every breath he took. She wanted him to have every advantage and pre-school was an advantage. However, the prospect of leaving him in a situation she could not control was unbearable for her. On the second day of school when I suggested that she leave the room, instead of feeling gratified that her child was ready, she took offense. She interpreted my asking her to leave as meaning that I did not like her because I let other mothers stay. I didn't realize that she had taken this attitude until weeks later when we discussed her enormous anxiety which persisted. As for Clifford, he was quite relaxed. In fact he seemed glad to be able to play without his mother's constant presence. He seemed comfortable enough to explore the room and he played quite contentedly. He was not a demonstrative child. He seemed to prefer to leave a dignified distance between himself and others and I respected his right to do this. I was receptive to him to the degree that I sensed he needed and wanted. I did not force my attention upon him. His mother interpreted this to mean that I did not "love" him. "If only I felt that you would love him, I would be able to relax.," she told me in one of our numerous and endless conferences. She haunted the halls for three months. I would open the door to take the group to the playground and there she would be, uninvited and unannounced, tears brimming over. She weighed every word and gesture of mine on some scale of her own. Her feelings could be compared to a wife toward the "other woman."

Clifford had some problems as might be expected of a child who had had no discipline or preparation for group participation, but separation anxiety was not one of his major problems. His mother, however, magnified his difficulties out of all proportion to reality and in her mind it was always because of someone else's refusal to accomodate to Clifford. She paced the halls of the school. She conferred with the director constantly. She cried. Finally she withdrew him from school. I think she subsequently went into therapy.

Johnny's case was more typical:

JOHNNY

At the end of the third week Johnny's mother was still in the building. She was getting exasperated with him and began talking about taking him out because he was not ready. I felt that he was ready but that he was just one of those children who needed more time. He was very much aware that he was the only one who needed to cling and he wasn't too proud of himself, but he couldn't quite bring himself to make the break. He played constructively and seemed relaxed except that every so often he had to go outside the door to see if his mother was still there. At the beginning of the fourth week, I felt that at last he might be ready but that he needed some special gesture of reassurance from me. I took him in my lap and read a story to him. I could feel his affection and growing trust. I told him, "Johnny, I think you are ready now to come to school like the other children without your Mommy. Tomorrow she will bring you and then go home. If you need her we will call her and she will come. When you are in school I will take care of you just as your Mommy does. If you need anything you can come to me. Teachers are something like mothers. Did you know that?" Johnny smiled a little and nodded his head. I could see that I had reached him. The next day he kissed his mother goodbye. He turned and then he called her back for one more hug. Then he let her go. From that time on he was fine.

CHAPTER 5 THE PARENT CENTER

The parent community room is an integral part of the Village School. Mothers and fathers congregate with other Village parents in an atmosphere of fellowship. It is a place where they can socialize over a cup of coffee and share stories with each other about their children. They come, also, to learn more about their young sons and daughters and to become a part of their school experience. When they pick up their children at the end of the day, each parent is eager to know what the child has learned that day and what activities are planned for the future. They want to know how their children are adjusting and whether they are making friends. They want to get to know the teacher and to make a judgment as to her ability to understand the children and to teach them the things that the parents value. They want to learn to be more effective parents and to make the best use of the time they share with them.

The room is cozy in it's decor with a sofa and upholstered chairs in a conversational grouping. There are several round tables and chairs. The walls are attractively decorated with pictures of parents and children sharing moments of loving closeness, engaged in joyful activity. There is a large bulletin board near the door on which are posted notes from each teacher briefly describing what activities the class engaged in that day. The note is a colorful form beginning: TODAY WE——— (The teacher writes:) ——*discovered that plants have roots. We dug up one of the lima beans that we planted 5 days ago. There were little white hairs growing out of the roots. Miss Jenson read a book to us called The Little Seed. In the playground we planted radish seeds. We also made apple sauce from a recipe that had pictures telling us what to do step-by-step. It tasted good.* The bulletin board also contains a list of recommended books on the subject of parenting pre-school children. There are announcements of seminars, discussions and speakers to be offered in the coming months. Messages are posted each week in large letters to catch the eye of parents which inspire positive attitudes toward learning and toward parenting. (GOD COULD NOT BE EVERYWHERE, THEREFORE HE MADE MOTHERS—Arab saying.) or (HEAVEN IS AT YOUR MOTHER'S FEET—Persian saying.) or (EVERYTHING I

NEED TO KNOW I LEARNED IN KINDERGARTEN—Robert Fulghum.) On the opposite wall are pictures drawn or painted by the children with their names prominently displayed. A telephone is available for the parents to use while they are present at school. There are bookshelves across two walls in a double tier placed at eye level. There is a table under the bookshelves in the corner featuring information about a particular book and it's author, which may be related to the current seminar, discussion group or speaker scheduled that month. The books lining the shelves are all on the subject of parenting, pre-schoolers, education or related subjects. They include titles of recently published books:

<u>The Preschool Years: Family Strategies That Work from Experts and Parents</u> by Ellen Galinsky.

<u>Hand-Me-Down Dreams: How Families Influence Our Career Paths and How We Can Reclaim Them</u> by Mary H Jacobsen.

<u>Connecting With Our Children: Guiding Principles for Parents in a Troubled World,</u> by Roberta M. Gilbert.

<u>Beginning With Books: Library Programming for Infants, Toddlers and Preschoolers.</u> by Nancy N. Desalvo, Faith Hektoen.

<u>Behavior Problems in Preschool Children: Clinical and Developmental Issues</u> by Susan B. Campbell.

<u>Breakfast Is Only the Beginning: A Fun-Filled Practical Guide to Keeping Up With Your Preschooler</u>. by Mark Yaeger.

<u>Choosing Your Children's Books: 2 to 5 Years.</u> by Valerie White

<u>Classic Children's Prayers.</u> by Alan Parry (Editor), Linda Parry (Editor.)

<u>A Cure for the Growly Bugs and Other Tried-And-True Tips for Moms: From the Mothers of Mops.</u> Mary Beth Langerborg (Editor.)

The Expert Parent: Everything You Need to Know from the Experts in the Know. by Bethany Kandel

Magazines with related articles are also in the shelves. A lending library system allows parents to borrow books for a specified time.

Presentations and discussions are held monthly in the evening hours or on Saturdays in the Parent Center in order to accommodate working parents. The topic for discussion is usually related to a subject of immediate concern to the parents. For example, a poster or flier might read:

> **Ellen Galinsky** will be our Speaker this month. Ms. Galinsky is the co-founder and president of the Families and Work Institute in New York. She is a leading authority and speaker on work/family issues. She was on the faculty at Bank Street College for twenty five years and has authored sixteen books. She lives with her family in upstate New York. Her latest book, **Ask the Children: What America's Children Really Think About Working Parents,** is guaranteed to break the frantic cycle of guilt and stress that often entraps parents.

All staff members are invited to attend any of these presentations, but a few are mandated on a rotating basis to act as hosts for the evening. Refreshments are served and everything is done to make the parents and the speaker welcome and comfortable.

The Parent Center is presided over by the guidance counselor. She or he facilitates discussion groups, introduces topics to be explored and makes arrangements for speakers to appear. Discussion groups are scheduled once a month in lieu of speaker presentations. Parents drop suggestions for topics to be discussed into a "Topic Suggestion" box for the guidance counselor's consideration. The counselor then chooses a topic for that month and proceeds to gather as much information on the topic as she can in preparation for the appointed evening. She compiles a list of volunteers from among the parents and teachers to participate in the discussion. Possible topics: Keeping Bedtime Happy and Stress-Free; Discipline for PreSchoolers; The Father's Role in Parenting; Fears Around Three, Four and Five; Preparing Your Child for a New Baby. The counselor acts as facilitator but allows the parents to share their thoughts and experiences with the group. When the discussion begins to wander from the main topic, she brings the discussion back on track. She offers reading materials on the subject and gives helpful suggestions and solutions. Her working hours are different from the teachers' in that she begins her day later and ends later so that she will be available to parents in the late afternoon and early evening for those parents who work. She is available by appointment to counsel parents about their children and, if convenient, spontaneously. It is the counselor who handles problems of behavior of the children when it is disruptive to the class. She contacts the parents when appropriate and offers help and advice. She has an office in the Parent Center which offers privacy for parents who wish it. The counselor is familiar with community services and makes recommendations for parents and children with specific needs. She and the Director act as liaisons between parents and teachers. She is also in charge of the lending library and she acts as a substitute when a teacher must schedule a conference with a parent who cannot come at any time but during class time.

Reports on the childrens' adjustment and interests are written by the teacher and sent to the parents four times a year. Each report is followed by a private conference at the Parent Center. Reports are never written in a critical tone and are decidedly non-judgmental. They simply describe the child's interaction in school, list his favorite activities, and present a portrait of his personality. The report is brief but informative. For example:

> Robin greets us every day with a big smile and a "Hello! I'm here!" She usually heads for the game and puzzle area and begins to play with enthusiasm. She likes to help others complete their puzzles and she sees to it that they return their materials into their proper places. She tends to be somewhat bossy when the others do not follow the rules. She will stand with her hands on her hips and state the rules in a loud voice. She is also the first to comfort anyone who is upset with a sympathetic hug. She is inventive and usually leads in dramatic play situations, suggesting roles and scenarios. The others respect her and like her. She is an attentive listener at storytime and participates in games with joy.
>
> Her paintings are very expressive and she uses colors boldly. She can mix the primary colors on her own.

The teacher-parent conference follows in a week or two after the reports are sent out. A schedule sheet is posted on the bulletin board and the parents sign up for a specified time convenient to both the parent and the teacher. Both parents are encouraged to attend. The parents have an opportunity to ask questions and to discuss anything that is on their minds. It is also a time for parents and teachers to get to know each other. Parents can state what their hopes and expectations are, confident that they will be heard and understood. This is a good time for the teacher to discuss any behavior problems that need to be addressed and to agree on solutions that are mutually satisfactory. Strategies for dealing with the problems can be decided upon. It is important that the teacher treads carefully on subjects that are sensitive to the parents' emotions or touch on private issues. For example, a child might be very open in school about things that are happening at home that are very private from the parents' point of view. He might say, "Mommy and Daddy yell at each other every night and I can't sleep." Or, "My Mommy don't love me." These are situations that are pertinent to the child's development and may have to be talked about.

The child may be feeling frightened, lonely or frustrated and it may affect his behavior in school. Since they are an important part of his life, they must be dealt with realistically. However, the teacher must not confront the parents in a hostile or judgmental manner. It is important for her to be sympathetic and helpful rather than authoritarian in her approach to the subject. Here is an example of this kind of delicate situation: There was a day in school when three-year-old Carlotta sidled up to me and fixed her big blue eyes at me and said, "My Mama don't love me." I was careful not to brush this away flippantly. Children have a remarkable capacity to interpret situations accurately, even at the age of three. I gave Carlotta all of my attention. I did not say, "Of course your mother loves you. All mothers love their children." What I said was, "What makes you think your Mama doesn't love you?" Carlotta replied, "My Mama don't cook for me, my Papa makes my supper." I looked deeply into her eyes. I knew there was more to the story than cooking. She went on shaking her head, "My Papa hugs me but my Mama don't." She was clearly asking me to do something about this situation. When it was time to write reports, I did not mention this incident in writing, of course. That would have been too abrupt and invasive. I wrote of Carlotta's interests, her quiet participation in activities, and described her sweet and gentle nature. I included in my description a quiet sadness about her at times. The mother came to the conference alone, which surprised me, since it was the father who usually brought Carlotta to school and who attended the monthly discussion meetings. The mother sat quietly, looking somewhat wary and expectant. She was an intelligent woman and she asked several relevant questions about our program. She was interested in our curriculum. She wanted to know if Carlotta would be ready to read soon, since she was so articulate and bright. I explained that it was not our policy to teach reading at the age of three or four and explained that our priority was more in the area of exploration of the children's world through play, using their own senses and broadening their experiences. I agreed that Carlotta was indeed a very bright little girl, but that she would not benefit from symbolic learning at this time. The mother held my report in her hand and asked guardedly, "What is this about Carlotta being sad?" I replied that Carlotta did at times appear to be depressed and that she looked to me for comfort. The mother asked, "Why do you think that is?" but looked as if she already knew the answer. She was, by profession, a clinical psychologist and quite intuitive. This was the moment to tell her what Carlotta had said to me. I related the conversation we had had word for word. Then I sat back with no further comment. I let the significance of it sink in. Her eyes filled with tears and she admitted that she knew on some level that Carlotta felt this way. She said that she did love her daughter very much, but that she was afraid to get closer to her. "She needs so much from me that it frightens me. I'm afraid she will devour me." She accepted what I had told her with thoughtfulness and dignity. As she turned to leave, she promised to explore her feelings further and to help Carlotta to deal with hers. The subject was not brought up again by me, but the mother did indicate, weeks later, that she and Carlotta were "making progress."

Parents are encouraged to act as aides in the classroom when possible, but it is important to do it by invitation on a carefully scheduled basis. They must be discouraged from barging in uninvited. This could prove to be extremely disruptive, especially if several parents decided to "hang around" at the same time. The rhythm of the routine would be disturbed and the children would be distracted. Contributions of snacks are gladly accepted and the contributing child would be very proud and happy to share with the class cookies made by the mother or that the child had a part in baking at home. Birthday parties, with a parent bringing the refreshments, party hats and favors are okay if scheduled for snack time and if it does not interfere with rest time or become too over-stimulating. These parties should be planned in advance by the parent and the teacher.

Special conferences can be arranged with the parents whenever they feel the need, apart from the four routine conferences. Rules about parents picking up their children on time must be strongly enforced with a special charge for overtime.

These rules are set and administered by the Director. She (or he) is the overseer of the Village School. She is responsible for execution of the program. She sees to it that the available space will be used to best advantage. She hires the faculty from among the best she can find. She is given an allotted budget from which she buys the best equipment and materials possible in order to provide the most effective and comprehensive program. She establishes the guidelines for the school and makes sure they are followed in accordance with her philosophy. She implements the standards for class size and teacher-child ratio. She also is responsible for hiring kitchen staff which cooks and serves lunch and snacks every day. She is the diplomatic liaison between the parents and the staff. She collects tuition from the parents and keeps the books. She must be intuitive and sensitive to the needs of the faculty and staff, the children and the parents in order to run a smooth operation. She enforces the rules, ameliorates problems, and inspires confidence in the program. She sets the tone and is the model for others to follow. The degree with which she fullfills this role determines the quality of the school itself.

References

Reich, Hans. Children and Their Mothers. New York: Hill & Wang, Inc., 1964.

CHAPTER 6 BRIEF HISTORY OF EDUCATION

Some understanding of the history of education is important in the planning of a comprehensive education program in order to gain a perspective on the past, to evaluate the present and to prepare for the future.

In the past, standards of behavior and the educational policies that accompanied them, were universal and consistent. Everybody believed in them equally. There was no room for variation so there was no confusion. At one time in the distant past, education was strictly the province of the church. The goal of education was to teach the Scriptures and to develop piety and obedience in children. Human nature was viewed as basically evil and children were seen as being in constant danger of being ruled by dark and evil forces in the personification of Satan. Non-religious education was considered to be the work of Satan.

In the seventeenth and eighteenth centuries a new view of the Universe emerged out of the scientific investigations and theories of Isaac Newton, Emmanuel Kant, Hegel and Descartes. Existence was explained in terms of scientific physical laws. Philosophy moved away from theories of divine intervention and religious doctrine lost it's influence over education. A new, more scientific view of human nature began to be espoused culminating in Freud's theory of personality. Freud saw human nature as being in constant struggle with the three forces within the individual: The Id, the Ego and the Superego. The Superego consists of moral standards adopted by the child from his parents. The Id consists of primitive biological forces that are aimed entirely toward pleasure. The Ego is the reality oriented dimension of personality which strives for balance. Science replaced religion as the basis for and the purpose of education. Paralleling this development in scientific philosophy, a new political philosophy began to take form. The American Revolution and the French Revolution loosened the old boundaries of tradition and loyalty to monarchs who ruled by divine right. Freedom and liberty became a new value. Self-direction and self-government became a new hope, then a goal and then a right. Human nature was no longer viewed as inherently bad, but good.

It was Freidrich Froebel who brought this philosophy to education and to the world of children. He saw in little children a divine spark of perfection and goodness which he believed could be nurtured toward a new and better form of life than had ever been known before. It was his belief that the loving mother (or kindergarten teacher) who respects the free activity of the child, who possesses an instinct deeper than thought, who is able to restrain her own self-will and to elicit voluntary obedience rather than demanding blind obedience, could instill in the child a consciousness of an underlying unity between God, Nature and Man. Through his self-activity and through the companionship and sympathy of an understanding adult, the child would learn the "universals of humanity" through a natural and spontaneous "inner connection."

Before Froebel, educators had studied children to learn what a teacher could do for them and to them. Education was regarded as a system of training children how to act socially and how to develop skill in executing assigned tasks in a prescribed way. Froebel regarded education as a process of growth within the child, a process which is the child's own work, done by and through the child himself. He believed that all education methods should be in harmony with the natural processes of the child's own evolution. The teacher role is to provide a stable, loving and stimulating atmosphere which is conducive to this self-directed work. Thus the child can develop skills in performing tasks at the same time that he is developing the power to act independently, to influence the outcomes of situations that affect him, to develop personal judgment, and to appreciate the natural laws of unity with the earth and God. If left to his work of self-activity with a sacred respect for his selfhood, the child would achieve his full potential for harmonious and responsible action. He would "love to do right rather than wrong." Froebel created his concept of the Kindergarten as an ideal society which would prepare a race of people for "greater, truer, purer, more successful living in the wider spheres of social and national life."

Thus, the child as a learner became more than just a gatherer of facts or a well-trained technician; he became a torchbearer of hope for a new and better world in which human beings could be self-directed, spontaneous and free. The forerunner of Froebel's thinking was the French philosopher, political thinker and novelist, Jean-Jacque Rousseau. His eighteenth century writings criticized the degeneracy of the contemporary culture and glorified the more primitive civilizations. Rousseau's notion was that the primitive man was a "noble savage." He was "natural" and therefore inherently good. The evil in man arose from the distortions of society. Rousseau also believed in the nobility of childhood and the inherent goodness of the child. He insisted that education be based upon the native capacities of those who were taught. There was a need to study children in order to discover what these native capacities and powers were. Rousseau's philosophy produced an impetus toward efforts for educational progress. It gave birth to the concept of freedom and growth as the true purpose of education. Education began to be recognized as a process of natural and spontaneous growth within the child, not as something to be forced upon him from the outside. It was Froebel who carried this seed of Rousseau's into the nineteenth century so reverently, and further nurturance of its branches were spread into the twentieth century by John Dewey and Maria Montessori. John Dewey also had a strong reverence for the state of childhood. He also viewed education as a process of growth. Rousseau's espousal of natural education against the formal doctrines that were prevalent during his time caused his novel Emile to be condemned as a revolutionary treatise. Dewey's espousal of the same natural education was ripe for acceptance. The time for a natural (progressive) education had come. Dewey advocated that the studies of a child should be related to his present needs and should grow out of his natural need to know and out of his natural need for self-preservation. For schools to impose adult material on children which is unrelated to their intrinsic curiosity is suicidal. It deadens their natural desire to know. Dewey thought that the greatest and commonest mistake that schools make is that they neglect to relate the material to be learned to real life situations in the experiences of children. In his view, schools of the day functioned on the assumption that the human mind is averse to learning. Such an assumption would be like assuming that the digestive system is averse to food and that it needs to be coaxed or forced to have anything to do with it. He believed that a hunger for learning needs to be kept alive. In order to succeed in accomplishing this we must be willing to be patient and allow children to learn at their own rate and in their own natural rhythms. Maturity is the slow growth of powers. Ripening takes time and must not be hurried in order to adhere to an adult timetable of some remote time in the future. Dewey's philosophy was expressed very simply in the flollowing statements: 1) Nature would have children be children before they are men. 2) Teach the child what is of use to him as a child. 3) To learn to think we must exercise our limbs. 4) Children are interested in the things they need to know about. Dewey wanted to put into children's hands the power to indulge their natural desire to know. He describes the kind of school which was his ideal. In such a school, children did not sit stiffly at desks facing the teacher, waiting for her to give them something called an education. They moved freely, exercising their bodies in the natural way of children. The curriculum consisted of activities such as physical exercise, nature study, music, handwork, field geography, sense culture, fundamental conceptions of numbers, dramatizations and games. Ideally much of the learning is done out of doors. The natural interest of children in games provides an opportunity for them to enjoy involvement in learning through games that require muscular skill, reading, writing and arithmetic. Active participation in productive activities such as building actual structures, either lifesize or miniature, involves measurement, planning, reading instructions and problem solving. Such activities provide experiences in learning that are quite different from merely reciting from a book in the presence of an authoritarian teacher. Children working real gardens, growing things, can learn more about nature through their own senses and experiences than they can ever learn in a static teacher-oriented classroom. Dewey believed that learning through experience was dynamic education and that it produced growth. This concept was called progressive education. Dewey understood also the importance of preparing the child to grow into the adult world. However, in order to take his place in society, he must be given the opportunity to learn the true meaning of the democratic system of government. The best way to learn anything, according to Dewey, is to internalize it through active participation and first hand experience. By living democracy and by practicing its precepts in his everyday life, the child will naturally grow into his role as citizen when he grows up. In schools where children are prepared to take responsibility for breaking down the barriers of class and race (and sex?) there can be practical application of democratic principles within the experience of children in their world.

Maria Montessori was the first woman to be granted a medical degree in an Italian University. Dr. Montessori never had an education course, but she became involved in the problems of schools from her work as the director of a school for the mentally retarded. In an attempt to help them with their school performance, she developed her own materials and methods which proved so successful that these "defective" children were able to pass public examinations for primary certificates, about as far as the average Italian of the day (1915) ever reached in formal education. Her philosophy was born of Rousseau and in many ways paralleled Dewey's. Yet there were some fundamental differences.

The core of the Montessori system was based upon three fundamental truths regarding the nature of children: 1) Children are different from each other and need, for their fullest development, the greatest possible liberty. 2) Children must learn for themselves in order to grow. The impulse to learn must come from within. 3) Under proper conditions children enjoy educating themselves more than anything else. These truths sound so much like Dewey that they might have been said by him. However, the remarkable difference between Dr. Montessori and other educators is that she logically applies these principles to fit her own system. The learning environment is prepared by the educator in such a way that it is easy for the child to teach himself. The classroom is organized and arranged to allow freedom of movement. The child uses the prepared materials and discovers the attributes within them for himself. He is free to develop and to work alone without interruption or intervention, absorbing what he finds along the lines of his own inner direction. Helpful learning experiences are made possible and those that are harmful are excluded. Factors are supplied which will satisfy the child's intellectual, moral and social needs and religious instincts. In such a prepared and controlled, orderly environment, the child as learner can grow toward independence and self-sufficiency. The concept of the authority figure in the form of the classroom teacher who motivates children to learn for fear of her or of her disapproval was slowly changed through the influence of such innovators as Rousseau, Pestalozzi and Froebel. But, the classic Froebelian Kindergarten with its protective mother-figure-teacher who inspired children to learn for the love of her was not Maria Montessori's ideal model. This change in the conception of the role of the teacher represented to her a kind of limited progress. She believed strongly in learning for one's own sake, to meet one's own criterion of success rather than learning for the sake of approval, even by a loved person. "Help me do it myself" was the message she seemed to get from the children she had seen. Her "directress" as she called her, was a "non-teacher" in the conventional sense of the word. This "non-teacher" used observations as her principal teaching tool. She was sensitive to the needs and the inner life of the child and knew how to respond to cues provided her by each of the children with whom she worked. She helped him or her organize his or her work and respected the life-in-process that the child's work represented. She provided the conditions for the child to be set free, but she also set limits. She guided him without imposing her presence too much. She was watchful, respectful, patient and non-judgmental of his spontaneous activities. She was not, as in Froebel's model, the filter through which passed all praise, all blame and all motivation. She did not interpose herself between the child and his experience. She respected his privacy and his independence. Montessori especially discouraged mothering tendencies in those teachers who used their role to satisfy their own emotional needs.

Those who became critics of Montessori's methods expressed shock and dismay at the idea of freedom in the classroom. What? A school without the rule for silence, for immobility, a school without fixed seats, without stationary desks, where children may sit on the floor if they liked or walk about as they please; a school where children may select their own occupations, where the teacher is always silent and in the background? Why that is no school at all. It is anarchy! And that is the crux of the matter concerning human nature. These critics in their hearts still believe that human nature is evil and depraved. They alone know what is good for others. They do not trust human nature to be responsible for its own control in the presence of liberty. They believe that anarchy is the natural result when the policeman lets down his guard. They do not believe in democracy, though they may give vehement lip service to it. They feel that it is well and good in theory. But, in actual practice in the classroom? Our democratic principles state that citizens should be granted the utmost freedom which is possible to grant them without interfering with the rights and freedom of others. However, it is a freedom within limits. Dr. Montessori never for a minute advocated anarchy. In fact her idea of liberty was not the same concept as the one understood by the northern Protestant countries around her. Montessori's liberty was that of Catholic tradition. It offers absolute freedom to do what is right. It reserves the right of authority at all times to determine what is wrong. Montessori reserved the right for herself to judge the good and evil in children's actions. In fact, Dewey himself feared that the Montessori method was too similar to conventional schools because the teacher was still the sole judge of what the child could do and that Montessori only increased the range of what was permissible.

Still, the rule in her school, like the rule in civilized society, was that no act was allowed which transgressed against the common welfare or was in itself rude or offensive. That children were free did not mean that they may throw books at each other's heads or light a bonfire on the floor, anymore than free citizens of a republic may obstruct traffic or ruin a drain into the water supply of a town. It means simply that they are subject to no unnecessary restraint and no meddling with their instinctive private preferences. Dr. Montessori's own school, the Casa dei Bambini in Rome, and others based on its model, are living proof that freedom and liberty do produce a respect for the rights of others and do foster self-discipline. Discipline problems simply do not exist in these schools, as they seem to in conventional schools. In an authoritarian atmosphere children might appear to conform but their behavior is contingent upon how well and how long they are controlled by an outside force. The minute they are set free they act out their resentment and rebel. Ultimately, discipline must come from a fundamental belief in the justice and order of the system, and in power granted by consent.

Dewey's fears proved unjustified. In fact, his principles of "progressive education" fell into disrepute when too many over-zealous adherents of absolute liberty interpreted freedom to mean license. Progressive classrooms all over the United States fell into absolute chaos. The aim of education should be to develop responsible individuals who appreciate and value the freedom, the customs, the standards and ideals that our democratic system represents. Personal liberty alone, without commitment to collective discipline for the collective good, can be destructive.

References

Dewey, John. Democracy and Education New York: Macmillan Company, 1916.

Dewey, John. School and Society. Chicago: University of Chicago Press, 1900.

Dewey, John and Dewey, Evelyn. Schools of Tomorrow. New York: E.P. Dutton & Co., Inc., 1915.

Feldman, W.T. The Philosophy of John Dewey . Washington, D.C.: The Johns Hopkins Press, 1934.

Fisher, Dorothy Canfield. Montessori for Parents. Cambridge, Mass.: Robert Bentley, Inc., 1965.

Froebel, Friedrich. The Education of Man. New York: D. Appleton & Company, 1887.

Hendel, Charles W. John Dewey and the Experimental Spirit in Philosophy. New York: The Liberal Arts Press, 1959.

Kocher, Marjorie B. The Montessori Manual of Cultural Subjects. Minneapolis: Denison & Company, Inc., 1923.

CHAPTER 7 TO DISCIPLINE MEANS TO TEACH

Discipline is a means of survival in an organized society. It teaches us how to behave in order to be able to live in the world with other people. It is the very heart of education. The best method to use in teaching this important subject requires careful consideration. Schools in general do not have a very good track record for devising or planning effective methods of teaching discipline. There is much misunderstanding concerning it's true meaning. Any educational program, at whatever level, must begin with an understanding of the nature and purpose of discipline. It is too important to leave to chance, which is too often the case. Too often it is left to the teacher's own discretion and is dependent upon his or her own personality or mood on a given day. This seems especially true as children proceed through the upper grades. The teacher reacts emotionally when her patience is depleted. The subject of discipline must be planned for before a crisis occurs. The administrator of the school must back up the plan in every way possible. We would not consider teaching the subject of advanced calculus without a plan, without a thorough understanding of its basic principles and without consideration for the readiness of the students for each step of learning. Calculus could never be taught at random. The subject of discipline is at least as important as calculus and is worthy of as much planning and preparation.

We must first agree on what is meant by discipline. To start with, discipline and punishment are not synonymous. This is an important distinction to make at the onset of a plan. Punishment means hurting someone in retribution. Parents and teachers will punish children to appease their own anger and impatience. Being human, they react to the child's behavior with emotion, based on how much the action inconveniences them at that moment. Punishment is for the purpose of "getting even." One punishes for one's <u>own</u> sake. It is understandable that parents will punish children out of exasperation at times. They are with them constantly and relentlessly and they are human. Their children will understand this on some level and forgive it. However, the teacher has a different relationship to the child. (She can sent him home at the end of the day.) She has an obligation to remain professional and a responsibility to teach him. Discipline as opposed to punishment is for the purpose of improving the child, of teaching him the acceptable way to behave in the world. The need to influence the attitudes and habits of young children is too urgent to be left to chance, or to satisfy the emotional needs of the teacher. This aspect of education must be carefully planned and controlled in the expectation that the best of learning will take place.

In our American society we seem to have lost our grasp on establishing clear and consistent standards of behavior that are workable and effective. We see around us every day rudeness, hostility and violence which is evidence of our society's failure to transmit ideals of conduct and social skills to the next generation. Where have we gone wrong? What are the values which prevail? Life in our society is far from simple. The community sharing common ends is so huge and variated that the task of education has become extremely complex. There are a variety of conflicting views concerning our basic human nature. Our perspective is colored by our individual religious beliefs, our race or ethnic origins, our political beliefs and our degree of education. There is not one clear collective consensus of opinion about what we expect of our children in terms of social behavior.

What we expect is determined by our view of human nature. Is human nature basically evil and destructive? Do we need religious intervention to save us from our natural tendency to evil? Are human beings controlled by subconscious forces consisting of primitive biological strivings which seek only pleasure and self-gratification? Or, is the individual inherently a social being struggling to find his place in society? Or, is human nature inherently benevolent, altruistic and oriented toward positive growth and self-actualization? Each of these beliefs have evolved historically. What do we believe today? Do we know? Each individual is free to believe as he chooses. Beliefs conflict and result in confusion when it comes to setting standards.

There is some evidence that Froebel, Dewey and Montessori have caused some changes in our educational philosophy. There have been some nervous attempts to put into practice their principles of freedom in education. Progressive education has been a failure because liberty has been misinterpreted to mean permissiveness; destructive behavior was tolerated in a dogmatic adherence to a quasi-religious fanaticism. To bend over too far backward in order to fulfill an ideal is to abdicate responsibility and suspend judgment. The experiment has gone awry and the pendulum swings back. In reaction to this over-permissiveness and in fear of anarchy there has been a trend "back-to-basics." The concept of the "traditional school" where "readin', writin' and 'rithmetic" are taught and where law and order prevail is the current ideal. It may mean that freedom in education is too difficult to deal with in a large, mass-produced educational system. It may mean that it is too inefficient in a society that values efficiency above all things. Montessori's schools were and are to a large degree voluntary and to a degree selective. She herself was prepared to expel those children who did not fit into the system by showing themselves to be incorrigible.

And so we continue to search for a workable system of education which will answer the personal needs of the individual child that is efficient and affordable in this complex, industrial, computerized, multi-racial, multi-ethnic, multi-cultural, capitalistic democracy of ours. In our public schools, children are again seated in rows facing the teacher, writing on worksheets, learning by rote, being expected to sit quietly and to obey. There has been some attempt to shift toward a more creative approach to learning. In elementary classrooms, children can be seen working on the construction of hands-on projects from time to time. But, there is so much to be learned in so little time that pressure builds up. Urgency and orderly procedure take priority. Efficiency takes precedence over concern for the natural and spontaneous growth of the individual child. Classes are larger than they should be due to economic and budgetary concerns. Discipline is based on some vague standard of expectation with swift punishment for infractions. The child is expected to know how to "behave" and to conform to the teachers standards of quiet and absolute order. A norm for the group is established in a way that leaves very little room for spontaneous self-activity or freedom of expression.

Teachers still have a hard time truly believing that children are inherently good. It is easy to understand why. Many children come to school from homes which are so deprived in so many ways that they have no concept of self-control. There have been such gaps in their development that they are unable to function in an orderly fashion. They have not developed a fundamental belief in justice and don't understand the need for order. They don't have enough faith in the system to be able to give their consent for the power of authority. They feel as if they are alone in a hostile, unfamiliar world and that they must defend themselves with whatever means are at their disposal. They have not been taught discipline with love and respect for their human dignity. Often their parents grew up as confused as they are. They themselves experienced only punishment as a means of control and know no other way. They are often too enervated in their struggle for physical survival to give much thought to learning new and better ways of teaching their children the social skills that teachers expect of them. The child enters school with poor self-esteem and without a clue as to how he can control the raging anger and confusion within him. It is an overwhelming task for the teacher to redirect his behavior. Allowing him complete freedom to indulge his own inclinations and to expect him to "do his own work by and through himself" at this stage of his development would be disasterous. He needs more structure not less. He doesn't know what his preferences in learning are. He needs loving, understanding control from outside of himself for a time to make up for the benevolent guidance he has missed.

Some of the children in the pre-school and in elementary classes are ready for the Froebel-Dewey-Montessori model. But, the teacher must aim to include all of the children in the group. She wavers between giving more attention to the ones who need the most help and structure and favoring the ones who excel in academic and social skills. She tries for some compromise in the middle. The struggle goes on.

This conflict is in itself strong evidence of the monumental importance of good early childhood education. Those children who have had good and constructive discipline at home will be truly ready for the Froebelian experience. They will prosper and deepen their own sense of identity. They will have a head start on self-fulfillment, self-sufficiency, self-control and self-mastery. They will develop a confident center within themselves that will help them adjust to whatever society will expect of them in the future.

The children at the other end of the spectrum who have not had the advantage of abundant love or discipline or the good care that they deserve can be provided with better soil in which to grow. A good early childhood program can begin to fill some of the gaps in their development if they are exposed early enough. They are still young enough to benefit. Day Care

Centers and Pre-Schools are not subject to the same pressures for achievement or judged by the same standards as elementary schools. They have the latitude and the means to make good things happen. All depends on the integrity, knowledge and concern of those educators to whom these precious young children are entrusted. Good, professional, purposeful preparation for this responsibility must be implemented in early childhood programs. Early childhood educators must be taken seriously and recognized for the important role they play as substitutes for today's working mothers. The prevalence of mothers of very young children who work outside the home makes it especially important to provide good care and education for their children. Even the best of schooling will never take the place of a mother's love, but we must offer the best care it is possible to give. Haphazard baby-sitting services in the hands of unqualified non- professionals are not good enough. This early stage of development is too crucial to be left to chance in the hope that it will turn out all right. It is time that early childhood education be given the professional status it deserves in the hierachy. It must be given the funding and the means to build caring and comprehensive learning environments.

Good constructive discipline is the foundation for a good education that will prepare an individual for life. To discipline is to teach. To teach is to discipline. Self-control of one's own behavior is the ultimate objective. In order for an individual to control himself he must believe in the system of justice which gives authority to those in charge. In order for him to develop this faith, the authority, and the system which supports it, must be trustworthy and fair. It must have absolute respect for the dignity of the individual. It must be direct and consistent. It must limit the undesirable behavior without attacking the individual's self esteem. In disciplining a child of any age, it must be made clear in the teacher's mind and in the child's mind that what is being criticized is his action and not himself as a person. A child's self image depends on what he considers his parents' and his teacher's opinion of him to be. It is relatively harmless to attack a child's actions which he can change. It is disastrous to attack his self-esteem, for he cannot change from being himself. There is a world of difference between the statements. "You are a bad boy for kicking me," and "Kicking me is bad and I won't tolerate it." Signifying to a child that his behavior is wrong by saying, "How can you be so stupid?" or "You're a mean, nasty, thoughtless brat!" makes him feel worthless and hopeless. It demeans the person not the act. The clear message should be, "Until you are strong enough to stop yourself from interfering with others, I will have to be the one to stop you." This can be conveyed by attitude, body language, facial expression, action or can be stated in words. "You may not throw things in this room." The lesson communicated in words should also be accompanied by action. A small child needs to be picked up and removed from the the arena of conflict. The biter is told to stop biting as he is being physically removed from the victim. He can then be redirected into a positive action. When he spills water on the floor, "Here is a sponge. Please sponge up the water you spilled" is direct and to the point.

It is also important to avoid too many premature explanations. They will just confuse the child. Once the teacher establishes her position as a respected authority, and she has planted in her students a belief in her wisdom and justice, it will be enough to simply state the expectation, remove the child from the situation and tell him what it is that he <u>may</u> do. The teacher would do well not to overwhelm the child with explanations as to why he must do or not do something. Initially, it is better to just state the facts. "Hitting will not be tolerated here" is a statement of fact. Overexplaining while the hitting is taking place is pointless and confusing: "Stop hitting because I am the teacher and I ask you to do this for my sake, for your sake and for the person you are hitting. Hitting hurts and if you don't want to be hit in return you must not hit." Explanations of discipline should come only after the child has mastered the fact that when the teacher asks him to stop hitting it is correct behavior to stop. Belaboring the point will only result in resistance. Properly teaching a child that what he has done is wrong consists of letting him know what is wrong and then dropping the subject until he makes the mistake again. Every time the behavior repeats itself, the same consistent message must be communicated. Inconsistent or contradictory discipline is far more confusing, and therefore harmful to the child, than extremes of too much or too little discipline.

Another method of discipline in order to achieve compliance is patient repetition. The teacher is persistent without resorting to nagging. Nagging is to repeat the same direction without taking any action, raising the voice until it reaches a crescendo of irritation. Patient repetition is saying "Stop, Johnny!" If there is no compliance or response, the teacher moves in and disarms Johnny, repeating once more, "Stop!" while physically enforcing the command. Children all too rapidly learn how often a teacher will repeat a command before enforcing it and will often wait for the umpteenth repetition of the request before believing it. On the other hand, they will learn to obey the first command if it is known to be followed by action.

There is no cut and dried formula for establishing the teacher's authority or for teaching discipline. The process is very subtle. The teacher sends out signals through the channel of her own personality. She does not control the children through fear of her. She draws them close to her because she is understanding, sympathetic, interested, helpful. She is firm when she has to be, but she is gentle. The children believe in her justice. She makes a convincing case for the desirability of decency and appropriate behavior. It is a slow, steady process of helping the children to see the sense of acting in socially benevolent ways. Finally the value of the rules make sense to them and become their values.

GUIDELINES FOR TEACHING DISCIPLINE

1) Establish your own authority by proving yourself to be firm but caring, fair and just.
2) Have absolute respect for the child's human dignity.
3) Criticize the action, never the child as a person.
4) State the rules and give brief explanation of the reasons for them.
5) Rules are not arbitrary and apply to all children equally.
6) Rules are just and appropriate to the age of the child.
7) State the expectation; follow with action by removing child from conflict; redirect him into constructive activity.
8) Be consistent and firm. Patiently repeat #7 every time undesirable behavior occurs.

Avoid——

1) Attacking child's self-esteem.
2) Over-explaining. This will undermine your authority by leaving an opening for excuses and manipulation. It sends the message that you need to over-explain because you are not sure of your position.

3) Inconsistency.
4) Emotional response
5) Nagging.
6) Sarcasm.
7) Yelling.

<u>Statements which are never heard in a good school——</u>

1) We've had just about enough of you.
2) If you want to cry, cry in the corner but don't bother the rest of us.
3) Don't come running to me with every hurt.
4) We can't wait all day for you.
5) I've told you a thousand times——
6) Labels and name calling: Crybaby. Show-off. Bully. Slowpoke.
7) Stop your whining.

References

Homan, William E. *<u>Discipline means "to teach."</u>* The New York Times Magazine, March 16, 1969.

CHAPTER 8 THE VILLAGE CLASSROOM

The classroom calls out to the children to explore, investigate, try themselves out. The games and materials provided have been carefully selected, planned to catch their interest. They are instilled with intrinsic learning concepts waiting for the children to discover through their own play. The teacher will be alert to any need for help, ready to answer questions when asked, ever on the lookout for safety, ever aware of what is being learned and broadening their concepts. The children will learn to play independently wherever and whenever possible. They will learn to use and then to return the materials in an orderly fashion. They will learn about shapes and forms and colors and sets. They will learn to enjoy creative experiences, to put their own ideas into visible form and to share them with others. They will learn to appreciate books and stories. They will learn to put their needs into words and learn ever better ways to communicate with others through language.

The Village classroom is carefully and thoughtfully arranged to accommodate various kinds of activities. Safety and convenience must always be of primary concern. The children have open access to the different areas of the room and to a large variety of materials during the free play period. Specific areas are designated for each activity. Each area has open shelves for materials relating to the activity so that the children can take what they need in order to accomplish their tasks independently. The teachers' task is to prepare the room every day in advance. The toys, games, paints, blocks, tools, clothes, books are in their familiar places so the children will know where to find them. Each of these items has it's place in the same position on the same shelf every day. The children will be taught to use one item at one time and then put it back in its place before they take another item. This will create order in the classroom and in the minds of the children, leaving them free of distractions and making it possible to concentrate on one thing at a time to completion.

THE DRESSING AREA

This area consists of cubicles or cubbies for each child's personal belongings. Each cubby contains a hook on which to hang a coat or an apron. Cubbies are low enough to the floor that the child can sit in his or her cubby if he or she wishes. The child's name is printed in block letters on the top and a picture (e.g. of an animal, flower, fruit) that the child can recognize as his own.

THE BLOCK AREA

The blocks are stored on the shelves sorted by size and shape. They are rectangles, squares, triangles, and arcs made of wood, large enough to handle with large muscle control, yet small enough to be of a weight a child can lift and use easily. Floor space is provided so that structures can be accommodated without interfering with other activities or becoming a safety hazard.

THE ART AREA

Four or five low easels stand with their backs to the wall with paper, paints, clear water and clean brushes ready to use. There is a long table with small chairs around it. On the shelves nearby are boxes of large crayons, paper, clay, scissors, paste, collage materials, each in their places. There is a walk-in closet to store materials in general which only the teacher has access to. The teacher may feature a specific art medium or activity each day until the children become acquainted with the materials and how to use them.

THE TABLE TOY AND GAME AREA

A long table and chairs dominate this area. Long shelves line the wall. Each game, puzzle, toy, set of materials is used in its turn and put back ready for the next child to use. The games and toys have been carefully selected for their intrinsic learning concepts, many of them Montessori materials.

THE LIBRARY AREA

Children sit on steps arranged in an arc and tiered theater-style. Pillows are lined up along the wall so that each child can take one to sit on or lie on. Books are on a book stand with the book-covers facing out and visible. For storytime, the teacher sits on a low chair facing the step-tiers. Every child can see over everybody's head. The teacher also has a flannel board on an easel nearby which can be used in story telling or games.

THE DRAMATIC PLAY AREA

Dress-up clothes hang on hooks. Jewelry. There are hats of all kinds suggesting role-playing (policemen, firemen, astronauts, mommies, daddies, teachers.) There are dolls, doll cribs and carriages, housekeeping items (broom, mop, play kitchen appliances, dishes, flatware, rollers), trucks, fire engines, table and chairs.

THE SCIENCE AREA

Might contain rocks, shells, starfish, plants, an aquarium, live animals in cages, magnets, prisms, a balance scale, a flashlight, a magnifying glass, pulley gadgets, a clock or any number of items which the teacher has inspired interest in.

THE WORKSHOP AREA

Woodworking tools may be provided under careful supervision. Snap locks, hook-and-eye locks, zippers, combination locks might be explored. Shoe shine kits. Silver polish and spoons. Anything that the teacher's imagination can assemble into a learning activity.

THE MUSIC AREA

Percussion instruments hang on hooks along the wall (Castanets, drums, cymbals, marachas, tambourines, rhythm sticks, triangles, wrist bells) A CD player with tapes and earphones are nearby.

THE OUTDOOR AREA

Planning for the outdoor area is often limited by the amount of space available. However, the illustration that follows is an ideal plan. It can be modified according to what is possible and what space and budget allow. Safety takes first priority in an outdoor program. It includes further opportunity for freedom of movement and spontaneous creative experience. The goal is to foster active large muscle development, exploration of nature, imaginative dramatic play, and exposure to fresh air. In the playground, the child experiences the natural world with himself as the frame of reference. He can climb into, out of, over, under, between, on top of and up and down. Feeling the elements: water, soil, wind, sunlight with his own senses, experiencing gravity, form, substance, movement, speed is studying science on his cogitive level. Equipment is unstructured so that he can use it in a variety of ways, limited only by his own imagination.

Ideally, the indoor classroom is open directly onto the playground with easy access to the toilets.

A fence completely surrounds the playground. It is substantial, sufficiently high and constructed in such a way that it does not invite climbing, nor does it allow for escape. This reduces the problems of supervision and allows for maximum movement in safety. There are two kinds of surfacing: grass and concrete and ideally, there is a tree that provides shade.

The entrance into the playground leads into the grassy area. A sandbox is there. It has an edge around it where the children can place their sand toys and where they can sit. There is a plank placed in one corner to use as a table for sand pies. A top is available to cover the sandbox overnight. The shovels, pails, strainers and sand toys are kept in a nearby closet.

A slide is placed in the center of the grassy area to provide plenty of room around it and to minimize accidents. The jungle gym is also placed in the grassy area in order to cushion falls. The jungle gym has dramatic possibilities as well as being good exercise. It can be a firehouse, a monkey house in the zoo, a jail, a rocket ship, etc.

The outdoor block area is raised slightly and forms a concrete platform, the floor of which is shared with the shed area. There is a storage closet for the large hollow blocks. There are no shelves in the closet because the blocks would be too large and heavy for the children to reach from above. The blocks are stored on the floor of the closet and stacked so that the children can reach them easily. The block area is on a platform in order to discourage the cyclists in the wheel-toy area from entering the block area. The one step up is small, child-sized.

There is a shed area covered with a roof and enclosed on three sides. The fourth side is completely open. The shed is used for shade on hot days and shelter on cold and rainy days. The shed contains boards, ladders, big boxes, rubber tires and barrels which can be carried or rolled down the ramp to the grassy area. The shed also has a table on which can be placed a variety of interesting materials: Pipes, ropes, nuts and bolts, and used car parts. The shed stores tricycles, wagons and other wheel toys which can be wheeled down the ramp into the wheel-toy area. This part of the playground is covered with concrete. There is room for 3 or 4 tricycles and a wagon or two. At the lower end of the concrete area is a water-table. The teacher will use discretion as to when it is appropriate to use. In warm weather, when bathing suits can be worn, it will have water in it and a variety of pails, funnels, squirt toys, spoons and measuring cups. The area might then be used for a shallow wading pool as well.. Water painting can be introduced using large paintbrushes for painting the walls with clear water.

The grassy area with the tree can be used in any number of ways. Barrels, tires, boxes big enough to sit in, ladders, and boards can be used creatively. There is an area for digging and one for serious planting. The grass may contain a row boat or a large undetailed box which the children can sit in and imagine into a car, train, boat, plane, rocket ship, etc.

CHAPTER 9 ACADEMICS AND THE CURRICULUM

The curriculum of the Village School contains all the seeds of future academics. It includes all of the same subject areas as do the higher grades: language arts, mathematics, science, social studies, physical education and the humanities. But, it nurtures intellectual processes that are on the cognitive level of the children and that are relevant to their current lives. Because they are not yet ready to read, does not mean they are not learning. There is much they can learn. It is serious work and must be taken seriously. It is extremely important to stress again, however, that children are ready to learn abstract concepts only when they have attained a certain degree of maturity, determined by nature's internal timeclock. To push them ahead too early into symbolism, before they have understood the relationship of their own bodies and senses to the world around them, is to do them a great injustice. We would not think of teaching algebra to elementary school children before they have mastered the basics of arithmetic. Children, like seeds, grow at their own rate, in their own time. A good curriculum will take this fact of nature into consideration. It will provide good soil to grow in. Early childhood teachers understand this. Sometimes parents do not. They think they are preparing their young children for future success when they hold up flash cards in the cradle. They are in a hurry to get to what they consider to be "real" education. Early childhood schooling <u>is</u> real education. It must not be looked down on condescendingly as "only play" and the teachers as "only babysitters." Play is young children's work. Teachers are educators and must be respected as knowledgeable professionals. The growth and development of our future generations are dependent on their knowledge and integrity and loving concern.

THE CURRICULUM

LANGUAGE ARTS

By the age of three, a child has learned a language that serves him in communicating with those around him. He has the ability to make his needs, thoughts and feelings known through words. The effort that he expends in mastering his native language and the ease with which he does it is amazing and admirable. Between the ages of two and five, he has a special heightened sensitivity to language that older children and adults have lost. He is creative; he invents his own patterns in much the same way that his distant ancestors began to build language. He spends the first five years trying to put existence into some kind of coherent form. The young child's knowledge of the world is limited and fragmentory, but he tries to bring order into it. ("Look, Mommy. I'm barefoot all over!") ("Is a knife a fork's husband?") ("The ostrich is a giraffe-bird.")

The young linguist likes word games, rhymes, nonsense words, repeated rhythms. He likes to create his own rhythms and rhymes. He'll say, "Clumsy Mumsy, " or "Salami Mommy" and giggle delightedly. He will chant over and over, "Over there, on the stair," and hop and jump as he says it. His rhymes and nonsense verse are full of joy and optimism. He expresses his feelings of happiness with himself and his world.

Fairy tales, fantasy and poetry are an essential part of learning. They strengthen a child's reality and emphasize it. They make language clearer, color it and underscore it. Storytelling, puppets, finger plays and songs also enlarge his receptive ear to language. Becoming engrossed in a story that is being told to him or read to him stirs his imagination, gives him pleasure, motivates him to want to learn to read for himself. Books open his eyes to wonder, to think and to dream. He learns that he is one in a community of people like himself and he gains a sense of belonging in the world. All this before he recognizes the symbols for words. Nevertheless, the road is being paved for appreciation of literature as he grows older and creates a hunger for books.

MATHEMATICS

Math is evident everywhere in the classroom. Cubbies stand in a row. If a child is absent and his cubby is empty, it is observed by the other children immediately; Johnny is missing! The table is prepared for six but only four chairs are there; How many chairs do we need? The children are standing in two rows facing each other: How can we make the rows even? The children are learning subtraction, addition, division, multiplication in concrete form. They add using buttons: 1 button plus 2 buttons gives us three buttons. They sort buttons into groups by color, size, pattern. They subtract lima beans: We have 5 lima beans. Take away 2 lima beans and we have 3 lima beans left. They divide the playdough in half: The same for Mary as for me, to be fair. They build with blocks and see and feel their shapes: they recognize a triangle, a square, a rectangle, a circle, an arc. They hear and learn the vocabulary of mathematics: a set of blocks, a collection of dolls, a group of girls, a pair of shoes, a class of children. The teacher reads stories about a flock of birds, a herd of horses, a pride of lions, a gaggle of geese. The children begin to understand the concept of sets. They begin to use the math terms repeatedly until they are part of their thinking process. All of these concrete experiences begin to be stored in their minds for future reference. Various games can be introduced to reinforce the concepts:

<u>Game</u>——"Bring Me——"

Children sit in a circle. Teacher asks Annie to bring a pair of blocks from the shelf. Annie brings 2 blocks and places them side by side on the floor in the middle of the circle. Peter brings a set of crayons. Jimmy brings a set of triangle blocks. Teacher asks Stuart to put back one member of a set of triangle blocks. Susie puts back 2 members of a set of crayons, etc until all of the objects are returned. This game can be played repeatedly until all children seem to understand the concept of sets as collections of things and are beginning to grasp the concept that sets are made up of members.

<u>Music Game</u>—— Song: "Karen has a pair of shoes" sung to the tune of "Mary had a little lamb."

Children sit in a circle. Karen sits in the middle of the circle as the children sing:

Karen has a pair of shoes
A pair of shoes, a pair of shoes
Karen has a pair of shoes
A pair of shoes today.

Karen goes back and sits in the circle. The child sitting next to her stands in the middle. The teacher asks, "What do you have a set of, John?" John: "I have a pair of hands." Children sing the song. Go around the circle until all the children have had turns.

Five-year-olds will be ready for these games:

Flannel Board Game #1

Purpose: To learn to define a set of objects and put them into brackets

Teacher: What do you see on this flannel board?

Children: Apples!

Teacher: How many apples?

Children: 3 apples.

Teacher: What would you call these apples when they are together?

Children: A bunch of apples/ a group of apples/ a collection of apples/ a set of apples.

Teacher: Let's take this red piece of yarn and make a circle around the set of apples so they can be together in their own place. (Child takes yarn and encircles the set.)

Flannel Board game #2

Purpose: To learn that objects can be members of a set and not be identical.

Teacher: What do you see on the flannel board?

Children: A rabbit, a cat and a dog.

Teacher: Is this a set?

Children: No!

Teacher: Why is this not a set?

Children: They are not the same.

Teacher: They don't look exactly alike do they? Is there some way in which they are alike?
Children: They are all animals.
Teacher; Could we say that this is a set of animals?
Children: Yes!
Teacher: What is it a set of?
Children: It is a set of animals.

Flannel Board Game #3

Purpose; To reinforce the concept of one-to one-correspondence.

One child puts a set of circles on the flannel board, another child a set of squares.

Teacher: Do the set of circles match the set of squares? We can find out by connecting them with these pieces of yarn. Yes, they match.

Flannel Board Game #4

Purpose: To learn that sometimes the members of two sets do not match. To learn the terms equal and not equal.

One child places 4 circles on flannel board, another 5 triangles.

Another child places yarn connecting each triangle with each circle. One circle remains unmatched..

Teacher; Do the set of circles match the set of triangles?
Which set has the most members?
How do you know the one set is larger than the other?

(Ideal answer: The number of sets do not match. They are not equal.)

Game of Add and Subtract.

Purpose: To learn the concept of one more member of a set and one less member of a set.

One child is called to come up to the front of the room.

One more comes up (Set 2)
One more comes up (Set 3)
One more comes up (Set 4)
One more comes up (Set 5)

One of the children sits down.	One less. (Set 4)
Another sits down.	One less (Set 3)
Another sits down.	One less (Set 2)
Another sits down.	One less (Set 1)
Lastone sits down.	One less (Set 0)

Game——Number Line

Purpose: To develop the concept of number sequence.

Place a line on the floor (paint it; use mystic tape or adhesive paper.)

Children jump from one number to the next backward or forward.

0_________1_________2_________3_________4_________5_________6

SCIENCE

A science experience for a young child is a combination of many kinds of experience: sensory, intellectual, emotional and expressive. He explores, examines and experiments. He looks, touches, smells, tastes with open curiosity. This curiosity can be nurtured and directed to a greater degree of awareness, observation and wonder. These are the basic attributes of the scientific method. A good science curriculum encourages active questioning. It provides opportunities for the children to explore a variety of materials so that they will become thoroughly familiar with their properties through their own senses.

The teacher's role is to set the stage for exploration, to peak the childrens' curiosity by introducing topics of interest, by helping to strengthen their awareness and powers of observation. To preserve and channel and develop a true scientific attitude that children have within them naturally is the purpose of science in the early childhood program.

Sensory Experiences

1- Science table has a tray prepared by the teacher containing materials of contrasting textures: sandpaper, fur, styrofoam, velvet, leather, satin, feather, sponge, absorbent cotton, burlap, flannel, cellophane, vinyl, felt, sheet cork bark. Two swatches of each. Children sort them putting together like textures.

2- Children close their eyes. Can you remember how a baby blanket feels? Is it rough or smooth? Soft or hard? Warm or cold? Other subjects: soap suds, walls, slushy snow, teachers desk, stiffly beaten whites of eggs, playdough, blocks.)

3- Identifying objects by touch. Prepare a box with a number of familiar objects. Child is blindfolded (or a large book is held in front of him so he cannot see.) Place one of the objects from the box in the child's hand. He guesses what it is. (Examples: chalk, pencil, crayon, block spool, paper clip, scissors, clay.)

4- With eyes closed, identifying objects by the sound they make. (Example: Stamping on the floor, poring water, closing a door, walking, running, jumping.

5- With eyes closed, identifying objects by odor. (Example; fingerpaint, soap, paste shellac, cookies, board eraser..)

Experimenting With Water

1- Drop various items into a fish tank (without fish) and observe them. Pebbles, corks, paper, pieces of wood, cardboard, buttons, etc. What will float? What happens when you blow on it or fan it? When you drizzle drops on it?

2- How can you get water from one pan to another? When you use rubber tubing, when does the water stop flowing? How can you make water move into something small you hold in your hand? Try a medicine dropper, a water pistol, a rubber ball with a hole in it, a rubber bulb clothes sprinkler.

3- Paint walls outdoors with large paintbrushes.

Weather

Observe and feel and discuss rain, wind, snow, sunshine. Express these in drawings, vocabulary, dance movements. Sing songs and listen to stories about the elements.

Mechanical Processes

1- How do things work? Compare effect of flashing beam of a flashight when it is focused close, or far, in the light, in a dark closet.

2- Observe the activities of the scale indicator as it varies with objects of different weight.

3- Demonstate a pulley on a line. Attach a pail, fill it with objects and move them along the line.

4- Play with magnets. What will a magnet pick up? What will it not pick up?

Growing Seeds

Seeds can be planted in: tin cans, old cups, styrofoam cups, flower pots, egg shells; they need soil, water and sunshine to make them grow.

1- Plant 10 lima beans in 10 half egg shells. Number each shell with a magic marker from 1-10. Put all shells in an egg carton. Water each bean in its egg shell and place the carton on a window sill in the sunshine. Water a little every day for 3 days. Watch the water soak into the soil. After 3 days dig up seed #1. How does it look? In 2 more days dig up seed #2 Does it have a root?

Dig up seed #3 on the 5th day. Does it have tiny white hairs growing out of its root? These are called hair roots. Day after day the roots and the hair roots push down into the soil. Watch for the bean seeds to push up out of the soil. How many days did it take? When do you see the seeds break open? When do you see leaves forming? How tall will it grow?

2- Plant carrot, radish, string bean or squash seeds in a special area of the playground. Observe. Water. Grow vegetables.

Cooking

Children and teacher bake cookies, make apple sauce, hot chocolate, etc. Children follow a recipe. They prepare ingredients, measure teaspoons, tablespoons, cups, etc. Observe how heat affects ingredients. They eat and enjoy their product.

Project: The Investigation of Objects

All About Balls

Children and teacher bring all kinds of ball-shaped objects from home: marbles, gumballs, cotton balls, baseballs, beach balls, rubber balls, a globe of the world, etc. Children are divided into sub-groups to study different questions about balls. One group studies the surface texture of each ball. Another measures the circumferences with string. Another group tries to guess what each ball is made of. Another group measures how far a ball will travel when it is rolled down an incline. Each group report their findings to the others. A discussion of ball games might follow and what objects are used to strike the balls (bats, mallets, hands, feet, racquets, etc.) Or a discussion about the earth, the sun, the moon being balls. Children draw and paint pictures of all kinds of balls. Their awareness, their vocabulary, their knowledge of a familiar object deepens.

SOCIAL STUDIES

Their experiences with the group will improve their social living skills. Their interactions with their peers and with the adults in the room constitute Social Studies on their own cognitive level. The classroom is a microcosm of the larger world. Everything that happens in the adult world happens in the classroom in the same basic structural form. The outward expressions and reactions might be different. The needs and emotions involved in their relationships to others are basically the same. Adults have learned to hide more, to deceive, to be "cool." With small children everything is out there in the open. They are looking for ways to protect themselves, to preserve their dignity, to feel good about themselves, as are we all. They are in the process of learning to understand and to respect the rights of others. Sharing, taking turns, not interfering with others, helping others, sympathy, empathy, compassion, respecting rules and authority are the elements of democracy. They must experience fair play firsthand in order to be able to put their trust in a system of justice. If the seeds of good citizenship are planted early they will blossom in time and will become an integral part of their personalities.

MUSIC

The children learn to experience joy in listening to music. They experience music in their own muscles, in the echo of their heartbeats, in the movement of their own bodies. They gain a feeling of security, of togetherness, easing social adjustments through music. They develop an ear for musical rhythms. They learn math, science and language skills to music. They learn simple musical concepts: fast and slow; start and stop; high and low; and simple rhythmic patterns.

They learn to use their own voices, singing songs. The school atmosphere makes the children secure and comfortable enough to listen to and participate in music naturally and freely. Songs are simple and chosen for their relatedness to the children's interests and experience. Records and tapes are provided of musical compositions suitable for rhythmic movement and improvisations: music for walking, running, swinging, jumping, dancing and for self expression in song play. The children experiment with musical instruments. Music becomes fun.

ART

The children are introduced to various art media, encouraging them to express their thoughts and feelings in a variety of ways. In their crayon drawings they can tell a story and record their perceptions. They paint, discovering the beauty of color and texture. They experience the sensuous pleasure of fingerpainting, and mixing colors. They discover that red and yellow makes orange, blue and yellow makes green, blue and red makes purple. They pound and roll and manipulate clay and play dough and find that they can make shapes of their own. They make objects out of paper and discover new forms. They cut and paste and glue together objects (feathers, buttons, lace, etc.) to make collages. They share their creations with others, tell their stories, bring them home proudly to show Mommy and Daddy.

References

Chukovsky, Kornei. From Two to Five. University of California Press. 1968.

Cohen, Dorothy H. The Learning Child. New York: Vintage Books: Random House. 1973.

Fraiberg, Selma H. The Magic Years. New York: Charles Scribner's Sons, 1959.

Gandini, L. *The Hundred Languages of Children: The Reggio Emilia Approach to Early Childhood Education. Norwood, NJ: Ablex ED 355 034, 1993.*

Katz, L.G. and Cesarone, B. *Reflections on the Reggio Emilia Approach.* Urbana, IL: ERIC Clearinghouse on Elementery and Early Childhood Education. ED 375 986, 1994.

Landeck, Beatrice. Songs to Grow On, New York: Edward B. Marks Music Corp-Wm. Sloan Associates, 1950.

CHAPTER 10 UNDERSTANDING EVERY CHILD

The good teacher goes out of her way to build intimate bonds with the children in her care. She wants to understand who they are, what they can do and how they feel. She gets to know their parents and siblings and the homes they live in so she will know the factors that influenced them to be who they are and why they behave as they do. She will observe them closely in order to assess and interpret their behavior so she can understand and be sensitive to their individual needs.

These assessments, observations and interpretations need not necessarily be formalized into a written report on every single child. It is enough to know the child and respond to him based on what the teacher knows and understands instinctively. The important thing is that she understands what makes him tick.

Here is a an example of a formalized assessment and evaluation of a child that was particularly interesting:

Assessment and Interpretation of Allison's Behavior.

Appearance and Description

Allison was three years old in September. She is a strikingly attractive little girl. Her hair is very light blonde, almost platinum. She wears it in a pony tail at the crown of her head while the lower part curls and waves softly to her shoulders. Her eyes are light blue and her skin is fair. She is of average height and weight for her age, neither too thin nor too chubby. She moves with agile quick steps and a feminine gait. She has excellent small muscle coordination. She always wears dresses and white panty-stockings. Her speech is unclear. She speaks a kind of lispy baby talk: "My Mommy binged dose shoes for me today." "Te tant have no djus." (She can't have any juice.)

Family

Allison's father is a producer of TV commercials. She has his coloring: fair skin, light blond hair, blue eyes. He has a mustache and wears his hair longish. He is attractively and conservatively dressed. He brings her to school every morning. He always appears quietly pleasant and friendly and he seems relaxed in his approach to his children. It was he who came to the parent-teachers meeting to get acquainted with the school and the teachers. Allison's mother works as a free lance interior designer. She is young looking and very attractive, with brown hair and blue eyes. She seems tense and remote much of the time and somewhat cold in manner. The other mothers have expressed their resentment of her unfriendliness. She never responds when Allison is invited to play at the homes of the other children in the class. Her attitude toward her children seems tense, almost defensive lest they demand too much of her time and attention. Allison's sister Katlyn, is five and is in the Kindergarten at Friend's Seminary across the street from our school. Katlyn looks like a mirror image of Allison, only slightly bigger. There is an African-American housekeeper who comes almost every day to pick the children up at school. She seems very warm and intelligent. The family lives in an apartment. The two girls share a room. They spend a lot of time in the parks and playgrounds. They have two white, fluffy cats, named Tucky and Vladimir, that look like feline versions of Allison and Katlyn.

First Home Visit

Before the opening of school in September, we visited Allison at home. We saw a lovely and unusual sight: two beautiful, blonde little girls sitting upon two clear, lucite cube-shaped tables, inside of which sat two perfectly white long-haired cats. Allison seemed very talkative and friendly. She curled up on my lap, brought toys and books to show us, and later spontaneously kissed us goodbye at the door. Katlyn, however, kept trying to out-talk Allison. Repeatedly we had to ask her to let Allison speak. Their mother finally had to ask Katlyn to please go to her room for a while so that Allison could speak to her guests.

First Days of School

Mother brought Allison to school on the first day, stayed fifteen minutes and left. She did not ask the teacher's opinion about whether Allison was ready. Allison was indeed all right that first day. She played freely and spontaneously with a number of things. It was the second day that she had a reaction. She wanted a toy that another child was using and she grabbed it away suddenly and aggressively. When I intervened, explaining that she could have the toy when the other child was finished with it, she had a tantrum. She cried loudly and would not stop. "I want my Mommy!" she cried over and over again. We called her mother at home in order to ask her to come to stay for a day or two, as the other mothers did. The housekeeper answered and said that the mother was at work but that she would call her and tell her to come to school right away. The mother arrived an hour later looking slightly annoyed. Had Allison misbehaved she wanted to know? She agreed to come and stay the whole time next day. She left after one hour, however.

Four Observations

The following four anecdotal records were selected out of many as being representative of Allison's characteristic behavior over a period of three months:

September 28 11:30 In the Playground

Today is Allison's birthday. She is wearing her gold crown with her name in glitter. She runs to the bicycle area and claims a bicycle quickly, leaving Sarah crying because she wanted that one. Sarah is taken to the "waiting" bench where she waits for a turn.

Teacher: "Allison, Sarah would like the next turn on that bicycle. Please give it to her when you are finished."

Allison: "No!"

Sarah begins to cry again.

Teacher: "Yes, Allison, finish your turn, then give Sarah her turn."

Allison puts her tongue in her cheek and quickly pedals away. She circles the yard several times watching Sarah out of the corner of her eye. Sarah waits patiently, watching Allison.

Sarah sees Hillary playing in the sandbox. She gets up and joins Hillary. They begin to laugh and talk. Allison looks at the empty bench on her next turn around the yard. She looks quickly around the playground. Her eyes rest on Sarah for a moment. Allison gets off the tricycle and runs to the climbing equipment. She climbs to the platform, four feet high, and, holding the teacher's hands jumps down into the grass. She climbs up again. She smiles as she stands on the platform. "I'm going to jump!" she giggles, then holds the teacher's thumbs tightly and jumps. She lands squarely on her feet, bending her knees and springing up for an extra little leap. She laughs. She climbs again to the platform. "I can do it myself!" she says. She bends her knees, preparing to jumps. Her eyes twinkle and she laughs in anticipation. She jumps with no help or support. She smiles, looking pleased with herself.

Teacher: "You did it all by yourself."

Allison: "Yes, I did it. Watch me."

She climbs up to the next level and slides down the slide. She slides three times. Each time she slides down she runs quicky to the ladder and climbs up again. Douglas, Jim and Rachel come to the slide. Rachel slides down slowly and walks deliberate steps around to the ladder. Allison comes down behind her sliding fast. She pushes her way past Rachel, this time coming down behind Douglas. She slides down quickly behind him so that she kicks him as she lands on his back at the bottom of the slide. He looks at her angrily.

Teacher: "Next time you slide down, wait until the person behind you is finished sliding, Allison."

Allison: "No!"

Allison runs around again to the ladder, pushing Rachel off the ladder.

Teacher: "Don't push Rachel away. Get behind her. Here, Rachel, you may go now. (Holding Allison back for a moment and allowing Rachel to go ahead.)

Allison tenses her muscles, frowns and sticks out her chin. She breaks away and climbs quickly up the ladder behind Rachel. At the top of the ladder is a platform from which the slide begins. Douglas, Rachel, Jim and Allison are standing there. Allison sits at the top of the slide. She sits for a long time. Jim and Douglas want to slide but Allison just sits and refuses to move.

Teacher: " Allison, slide down. The others want to slide too and you're holding up the line."

Allison: (Folding her arms over her chest and frowning) "No!

Teacher climbs to the platform. She puts her hands on Allison's waist.

Teacher: "You can't sit here this long if others want to slide. Now slide down so the others can have a turn."

Allison: "No!" (Frowning more deeply.)

Teacher: "I'll have to take you off, Allison." (Putting her hands firmly under Allison's armpits.)

Allison: (Almost screaming) "No!"

She holds on tightly to the sides of the slide. Teacher pries her hands loose and removes her. Allison screams piercingly and kicks her feet, kicking Jim who is standing nearest to her on the platform. Jim's face gets red. As Allison struggles and kicks, her birthday crown falls off and lands on the ground below the slide. Allison screams, looking down at her crown. "My crown!" she cries, her hand outstretched toward it over the side of the platform. Douglas slides down followed by Jim. Allison slides down after Jim and runs to retrieve her crown. Douglas gets there first, picks it up and puts it on his head. Allison screams and grabs for it, hitting Douglas. Jim punches Allison in the stomach. Allison screams loudly, doubled over. The teacher has been scrambling down the ladder during all of this and has to run around the equipment to where the children are. She picks up Allison, gets the crown and gently rocks her.

Teacher: "Where does it hurt, Allison?"

Allison: "My tummy. Jim punched me in my tummy."

The teacher holds her and tries to soothe her. Allison cries, "I want my Mommy," over and over and over again.

Teacher: "I know— you're hurt and you want your Mommy. I know."

Allison cries and cries and does not stop for ten minutes, not from the pain of the blow but just because she is worked up.

Allison's mother arrives at the playground to pick her up. Allison is still crying. The teacher hands her out of the gate to her mother. Her mother squats down and listens as Allison tells her story. The teacher lets the others out of the gate as the other mothers arrive. Allison's mother comes to the gate to talk to the teacher. Allison has finally stopped crying.

The teacher asks the mother to please wait until all the children have left. Then she turns to Allison's mother who says, "I want to know exactly what happened. Who punched Allison and why?" Her face is hostile and her blue eyes are icy cold. The teacher calls over the assistant teacher and together they try to piece the events into one whole truth. Allison's mother relaxes a little after we tell our story. She seems to be considering the possibility that Allison had some part in provoking the attack. She tells us the version of the story that Allison told her: "The boys took away my crown and punched me in the stomach."

October 15 9:30 Free Play

Allison is playing in the doll corner. She picks up a small blonde doll and puts it into the doll carriage. She covers it with a blanket. She takes a large black pocketbook from the shelf and begins to fill it with jewelry from the drawer. The pocketbook is on the floor as she does this. Her right hand is holding tightly to the doll carriage as she loads the jewelry in with her left hand (she is left handed.) Her eyes keep moving from the pocketbook to the doll carriage to the other children in the room. Hillary walks toward Allison. Allison stands up quickly and puts both hands on the carriage, looking intensely at Hillary. Her face begins to form a pouty expression as she quickly picks up the pocketbook from the floor and puts it at the foot of the carriage. She wheels it away from Hillary, giving her an almost inaudible (but triumphant) "Hmph" as she goes past, tossing her head ever so slightly. She wheels the carriage to a far corner of the room, pulls up a chair beside the carriage and sits down on it. She puts the pocketbook on the floor beside her, takes out the doll and rocks it gently in her arms. She sings in a lispy voice, "Ah, baby, baby baby. Sleep baby, sleep baby, baby, baby." Her little song is original, rhythmic and she sings it with real feeling, closing her eyes now and then. She walks around her corner of the room holding the doll and rocking it. Sarah comes toward her. They stand looking at each other for a few minutes. Allison holds her doll tightly to her. "You won't take away my dolly?" she asks, her blue eyes wide and questioning, leaning over a little and looking directly into Sarah's eyes. Sarah says, "No," shaking her head reassuringly, "I'll get another doll." Sarah runs to the doll corner, picks up another doll and brings it to where Allison is playing. They smile warmly at each other.

November 9 11:00 Storytime

The teacher sings, "Everybody sit down, sit down, sit down; everybody sit down just like me. Cross your legs just like Allison, cross your arms just like Sarah——————." Allison sits up tall, her arms and legs crossed, her face flushed with pride and pleasure to be the first one ready. The story is Green Eyes, a story about a white cat with green eyes. Allison's eyes are wide with excitement, her lips are pursed and she looks as if she will explode with the wonderful news: "I have a cat. I have two cats. That's Tucky and Vladimir!" She jumps up and points to the book. "Yes," says the teacher. "Allison has two white cats that look like this. She takes Allison's hand and gently leads her back to the floor. Everyone quiets down. The teacher reads. Everyone listens with great interest and absorption except Larissa (as usual,) who is moving and creeping around. She teasingly puts out her foot and pushes Allison's hand with it. Allison pulls away, frowning angrily at Larissa. Allison creeps up to Larissa and pushes her. The assistant teacher takes Larissa in her lap. Sarah moves and sits in Allison's former spot on the floor. Allison returns and sees this and pushes Sarah. The teacher picks up Sarah without speaking and places each child where she originally was, picks up the book and continues reading. Allison is not listening now but keeps glowering at Sarah. She sits as close to her as she can manage and pushes her with her hip. Sarah pushes back. The teacher takes Larissa and the assistant teacher gets between Allison and Sarah, picks them both up and tries to move them to the back of the seated group so as not to interrupt the story or obstruct the view of the book. Allison begins to scream, "No, let me go," and she folds her arms over her chest and fights being held. She breaks free and runs to "her" place and sits there continuing to scream.

Teacher: "Allison, we can't read the story if you scream. You may stay there if you are quiet."

Allison screams louder, kicking and throwing herself around.

Teacher: "Allison, if you can't stop we'll have to take you out of the room."

She continues her tantrum. The assistant teacher takes her out of the room as she kicks and screams. As we read the last page of the story, she is brought back somewhat recovered. The teacher puts an arm around her and lets her stand next to her for the end of the story. The others get up and get dressed. The teacher sees by Allison's expression that she is repentent and that she regrets missing the story. Her eyes are downcast, her finger is in her mouth—she is waiting for the teacher to make some gesture of conciliation. The teacher gives her a hug and says gently and casually. "I'm sorry you missed the story, Allison." Allison relaxes, she gives one final sigh and nods her head. The teacher looks into Allison's eyes and says, "Next time we read Green Eyes maybe you'll be able to listen instead of crying. I'll try to help you to listen, OK? It doesn't matter where you sit, does it?" Allison's eyes are full of warm affection now. She nods her head and then cuddles up.

December 3 8:50 Free Play

Allion is the first one to arrive. The teacher has flour, salt and food coloring ready to make play dough. Allison hangs up her coat quickly and runs to the table. She says excitedly, "I wanna help. I wanna help." She fills the measuring cup with flour and dumps it into the bowl. She fills the cup again and then again

Teacher: "Now salt, Allison."

She fills the cup quickly and excitedly with salt and pours it into the bowl.

Teacher: "Now fill the cup with water."

Her movements are quick, but she seems to be making a conscious effort not to spill the water and walks deliberately and slowly balancing the water in the cup. She looks as if she will just dump the whole cup plop! into the bowl.

Teacher: "Not yet, Allison, let's put the color into the water first."

Allison: "OK. Let me do it!" She pours in four drops as we count.

Teacher: "All right. Now let's pour it in."

She dumps the blue water in plop! and it splashes. She mixes and mixes. She smiles broadly, her face full of happy excitement. "Mix, mix," she says. When the dough is ready she begins to take chunks of it and (without suggestion from the teacher) begins to place a chunk of dough on the table in front of each chair. The pieces are pretty equal in size. She then runs to the shelf and takes the box of rollers, places one at each place on the table. She runs to the housekeeping corner and gets large flat plates and puts one at each place. There are still two places (out of six) without plates. She goes back to the housekeeping corner and brings back the correct number of plates and finishes preparing the table. She sits down and begins to play happily with the dough.

A Word Portrait of Allison

Words like relaxed, passive, phlegmatic, timid could never apply to Allison. She is at the other end of the scale. She reacts to life with enormous vigor and with total involvement. Her emotions are incisive and in full bloom and she does not inhibit their full expression. When she is happy, she is delightful: she glows, bubbles, laughs out loud. She plays with such pleasure and concentration. She will look up and if she meets the teacher's glance, she will break out into a warm, fourteen-carat smile. She is creative and capable and well-organized in her play. Her paintings are lovely; she uses clear colors, knows how to make the secondary colors herself. Her brush flows freely; she has good control and creates her own interesting effects. She wants to be part of everything that goes on and she wants to be there first: "Let me—! "Watch me!" "Show me how—." She is like a bass violin being played on the higher strings in a lively tempo. Her mood may change suddenly, however. Some small incident or frustration will trigger a negative reaction—an over-reaction. Her emotions sweep over her, run away with her. She is out of control. She screams, cries, kicks. No amount of reasoning can reach her. She can be maddeningly stubborn and inflexible. She can be so rigid in her determination to stand her ground that she sometimes frightens herself because there is no retreat. She can be whiny and irritable and deliberately disruptive. She is aggressively competitive. She must be first; she must be the one to hold the teacher's hand in circle games; she must have the blue bicycle first every day. She always seems to feel that someone is about to take something away that is rightfully and exclusively hers. She's always on her guard. She is fighting for her little place in the sun.

What Does Allison's Behavior Mean?

Some of Allison's high-strung, emotional behavior might possibly be due to genetic disposition. Children are born with a certain basically genetic personality structure. The way their parents and other key persons in their lives react toward them further affects the form the personality takes and the behavior that results. Where genetics ends and environment begins is difficult to determine, since it is usually the parents who provide both in the first years. Attitudes, emotional patterns, tensions can be absorbed like osmosis through the physical contact, facial expression, muscle tension. Body tension or body relaxation can speak louder than word-language to a small child. In a thousand forms of non-verbal communication, the parent transmits messages, emotions, attitudes, expectations, to the infant and child. Allison's mother is a tense person. Speaking with her one can feel the tension in her muscles, in her facial expression.

One can sense the defensiveness in her cold, blue eyes. This is the first reflection of the world that Allison ever saw. It is clear that Allison's mother is immature and uncertain in her role of mother. She resents having to give of herself to her children. She is frustrated because she cannot completely and freely pursue her career. She does not make an even superficial attempt to cover up her annoyance and irritation when Allison's (and Katlyn's) needs and demands interfere with her own. We had a Christmas party during which the children were to present their parents with the gifts they had made. We stressed to the parents the importance of being there—first with letters and then by personal reminders. Allison's mother brought her that morning, looking harassed and annoyed, making no attempt to cover up her impatience. She snapped, "I was told to be here at 9 o'clock." Teacher: "No. You were asked to be here at 11:15." Her face registered almost rage. She never bothers to read our letters—she always says she didn't get them. She stalked out unable to control her anger at having been made to lose her precious time. She returned at 11:15 and sang some carols with us. She could not wait, however, until Allison's turn came to present her mother with her gift. She left just as we were beginning to give them out. She left Allison to be taken home by the housekeeper.

Allison is subject to two extreme reactions from her mother. On the one hand is the reaction described above. She is remote and defensive, as if she is afraid that Allison will devour her if she allows her to get too close. She keeps her at arm's length. Allison's frustrations, her rages, her tantrums, are an expression of her need to be first with Mommy, first before Mommy's career. Allison replays this conflict in the classroom. Her behavior says, "I will be first somewhere with somebody. If I can't be first with somebody, I will hold on to things and have them first." Still, Allison knows that she dare not come too close to her mother. She senses that Mommy will allow so much and no more, and so she has, to a certain extent, adjusted to not having her mother there because she has had to. Allison does not overtly display a dependent attachment to her mother. When her mother leaves her she does not cry, but turns away and busies herself, as she did the first day of school. It is when she feels frustrated and hurt that the dam breaks and all her unanswered needs surface. Then she cries,"I want my Mommy, I want my Mommy." The other extreme reaction that Allison is subject to from her mother is a kind of subtle permissiveness and overindulgence. Her mother feels guilty for her limitations as a mother, and so she indulges her in ways that reinforce the temperamental behavior. She gives in to Allison if she screams long enough and loud enough. For one thing, she cannot give enough of herself to come to terms with the problem realistically; it is easier to walk away from it. For another, she projects her own feelings into Allison. In a way, Allison is herself all over again. When she indulges Allison's temperament, she is in a way indulging herself. Allison senses that by behaving as she does, she is fulfilling Mommy's subconscious wishes and at least here she is pleasing her mother.

Fortunately, Allison's father provides an alternate perspective of the world. When he smiles, one can see Allison in one of her sunny moods. He is relaxed with her and he is interested in her problems and in her development. He, not his wife, comes to all school meetings. He listens to our dissertations with interest. He asks questions that reveal his concern. He appears to sense the gap between Allison's emotional needs and her mother's inability to satisfy them. He tries to fill the gap as best he can. Allison adores her father. It is apparent by the way she moves in his presence and in the confident toss of her head that she feels adored by him. But then, Mommy is between Allison and Daddy, so she is not entirely first with him. Allison says, "Mommy is pretty but she has brown hair." (Not blonde like Daddy and me.) And then, there is also Katlyn. Her relationship to her sister is also a key factor in Allison's ego development.

Katlyn is so much like Allison in every way, only Katlyn got there first. They look alike: same basic features, same color and texture of hair, same hairstyle. They even wear the same clothes, twin-style. Except that Katlyn is two years older!" She is just bigger enough, stronger enough, and more developmentally capable enough to be always two jumps ahead of Allison. She out-talks Allison, whose speech is sometimes difficult to understand. She monopolizes the spotlight. She moves faster. In the face of all the competition and the frustration it must engender, Allison's spunk is enormously admirable. She hasn't given up or given in to this imposing, dominating giant of a sister—she is fighting and holding her own, some of the time. She is determined to be a person in her own right. When she sits at the top of the slide with her chin stuck out, her face in a determined grimace, holding on to the sides of the slide with all her strength, she is reacting in the only way she knows in order to be herself. She knows that she sometimes goes too far and it frightens her. She doesn't know how to stop herself or retreat and so she cries louder. She knows that a tantrum is not the best solution, but it is the only one she knows. It is like a call for help. Allison's behavior seems to say, "Notice me! I am here! I am important! Help me to become as big and as strong, as capable as I want to be (as my sister is.) Help me to control myself and to like myself better.

What Allison Needs in Order to Alter Her Behavior.

Allison needs——

1) A gentle and understanding authority figure who will support Allison's need to be herself; someone who will respect her dignity and will be able to cope with her tantrums, stubborness and irritibility without losing her own cool perspective and without indulging her.

2) A firm, consistent and supportive discipline which is clear, fair and not tinged with personal animosity or emotionalism—a discipline that clearly states, "You may not interfere with the rights of others. If you cannot follow this rule then I am here to help you do what you cannot yet do by yourself. We all like and respect you and we expect you to feel this way about others. By the same token, I will protect you from being hurt or interfered with by others."

3) Maximum opportunity to experience satisfaction in doing things and sharing experiences with others; an atmosphere that is conducive to rich and constructive learning.

4) Affection, acceptance and appreciation of her uniqueness, her talents, her positive qualities. This will help her to unfold in confidence and security toward a greater independence, spontaneity, creativity and self-discipline.

5) Freedom within a framework of order. A good structure with good firm rules will clear the way for creative self-expression. Such a structure can free Allison's inner self from chaos and uncertainty. From the freedom to create things her own way will come satisfaction, pride and a feeling of self-worth.

Allison's Progress Over a Period of Three Months.

Allison has made considerable progress. Her tantrums are becoming fewer and last for shorter periods of time. She smiles much more often. She is more relaxed and trusting of adults. We can often head her off now before the tempest breaks. She is so relieved and grateful if we can find some way to prevent her from losing control. Everything she does she seems to do with more satisfaction and enjoyment. It has helped Allison, too, that the housekeeper, observing the way she is appreciated and respected in school, has begun to follow suit. She doesn't show the same hopeless exasperation when Allison has a tantrum. She is more patient with her. Allison has blossomed.

References

Moustakos, Clark. The Authentic Teacher Sensitivity and Awareness in the Classroom. Cambridge, Mass: Howard A Doyle Publishing Company, 1966.

CHAPTER 11 MAKING CONNECTIONS

The first three years of a child's life are critical to the development of it's brain. This development begins before birth. Even in the womb, ten or twelve weeks after conception, nerve cells in the brain are actively making connections with other nerve cells and transmitting signals, causing bursts of electrical impulses. These pulsating waves and currents move and shift in ways that change the shape of the brain and foreshadow patterns that will enable the infant to perceive and interpret what he sees and hears when he enters the world. Neuroscientists are discovering that the physical structure of the brain is actually formed by the rhythmic firing of these neurons and the electrical activity which results from this process. The same process continues after birth, wiring the brain, laying out circuits for an explosion of learning. The brain retains those circuits that are needed for the development of language, vision, hearing, etc. Through sensory experience, the brain determines which of the billions of connections between neurons will be retained. Those circuits that are seldom used are eliminated by the brain in a kind of pruning process. By the age of ten or earlier, patterns of thought and emotion have left their imprint on the developing brain. The amount and degree of environmental stimulation the child's brain is exposed to determines which and how many active neurons are retained. The richer the experiences the child has, the richer the brain. The brain that is deprived of stimulation through rich experience retains fewer of the connections between the neuron cells and grows less. Children who are rarely touched and who are not given the opportunity to play constructively develop brains that are twenty to thirty percent smaller than normal brains. They are at a distinct disadvantage in the world.

"There is a time scale to brain development, and the most important year is the first," according to Frank Newman, president of the Education Commission of the States. The circuits that govern emotions are one of the first to be constructed by the brain. By about two months of age, the infant brain produces complex emotions such as joy and sadness, envy and empathy, pride and shame. These become emotional patterns depending on the type of emotional stimulation the baby brain receives. Neglect and abuse can cause brain wave patterns to develop that produce anxiety and stress in the infant. These suppress happy feelings such as joy and other light-hearted emotions. These unfortunate infants may develop "sad brains." If their caregiving situation is reversed within the first year, the chances of reversing the damage is favorable. Many scientists believe that there are sensitive periods in a young child's development when certain types of input are necessary and crucial for establishing and stabilizing certain long-lasting structures in the brain. These "windows" present themselves and unfold according to a strict biological timetable. If this input does not occur at this crucial time the window may be shut permanently for a particular brain pattern to establish itself. Children in this respect are like the birds who cannot master their song unless they hear it sung at an early age. In zebra finches, for example, the window for acquiring their song opens 25-30 days after hatching and closes after 50 days. By three years of age, the damage done to the brain of a child who has been neglected or abused is difficult to reverse.

The fact that early childhood experiences are crucial to child development comes as no surprise to physicians and educators. However, their awareness of this truth has, until now, been based on anecdotal observations only. Two studies, one by the Families and Work Institute in 1997 and the Carnegie Report in 1994 agreed that the first three years of a child's life are the most critical in a child's brain development. Now, neuroscience is providing hard new scientific evidence that can be verified under a microscope. In April 1998, the National Institute of Child Health and Human Development released a report stating that the best kind of day care can enhance the language and cognitive development of a child and increase his potential for success in school.

This realization has profound implications at a time when mothers spend so much more time in the workplace and less time with their children. It is more important than ever that parents make an effort to find the time to cuddle their infants, talk to them, provide them with stimulating experiences. If they are not able to be there for the child during the day, it is of major importance that they appoint a substitute who is qualified to fill the gap adequately. Quality Day Care personnel and teachers of early childhood programs must be trained and made available in large enough numbers to meet this growing need. The time is now to set our priorities as a nation for the good of our children and the generation to come.

It can be done if we organize our values properly and realistically and invest our interests and taxes where they will do the most good. When Hillary Rodham Clinton visited France, she observed one of the best day care systems in the world in action. When she asked a French government official why the French government had elected to spend so much money on child care, his response was."How can we not? These are the future citizens of France."

References

Nash, J. Madeleine. *Fertile Minds.* Time, Feb 3, 1997.

CHAPTER 12 OUR FUTURE CITIZENS

Where do we stand as compared to France in providing for the future citizens of the United States? Very poorly indeed. In fact, this country's day care provisions are anywhere from fair to terrible. A 1997 report by Yale University found that six out of seven day care centers were rated mediocre to poor. One out of eight were judged to be potentially unsafe and unhealthy. In another 1994 survey, the environments of a third of home-based care facilities were considered detrimental to the development of the children they serve.

This is a quote from an article clipped from my local newspaper on the very day of writing this chapter: The Arizona Republic Friday, January 14, 2000

By Christina Leonard and Judi Villa

> A Mesa day-care center was temporarily shut down this week because of persistent and multiple safety violations that put children at a "substantial risk of harm" court records show.
>
> In a rare move, the state Department of Health Services obtained a temporary restraining order against Tots Unlimited, 848 S. Alma School Road, citing problems ranging from improper supervision to uncovered electrical sockets in the playroom.
>
> The most serious infraction, they say, involved a 2-year-old who walked away in December and wasn't missed for 45 minutes.
>
> On Dec. 7, Maurice Davis, 2, apparently climbed over a fence.
>
> Employees didn't realize he was missing until the director spotted him with two men at a nearby grocery store.

This is just one example of the worst kind of facility. An overview of the day care situation in general reveals that in addition to the cost being high, too many caregivers are unqualified, health and safety standards are uneven and educational opportunites are lacking. In far too many day care centers, infants are left alone for hours in a crib staring at nothing. They are attended to only when their diapers need changing or when they cry. They are not receiving the attention they need that would bind them to adults or to the world around them. They do not receive the necessary stimulation to establish those neural pathways that form the brain and enhance learning and healthy emotional development. By kindergarten, it may be too late. If the child reaches the age of three without the individual attention and stimulation he needs he will have fallen behind and the window will have been closed.

What does this mean to us as a nation? Seventy percent of mothers work at jobs outside the home. The new welfare laws have forced thousands of others into the workplace. Who is to raise and nurture their young children? The need for affordable, high-quality day care has never been more immediate and urgent. There is too much at stake. A generation of socially and intellectually impaired individuals is too high a price to pay. How can we not provide universal top-notch care for our future citizens in the richest, most powerful country in the world?

Unfortunately, funding for child care does not rate among the highest of priorities with our legislators. These Americans seem to regard day care with a certain amount of distaste. Underlying and often unconscious Puritan values categorize subsidized day care as a service that allows mothers to work and therefore to neglect their children at the expense of the government.

They consider day care the responsibility of the parents. Conservatives long for the days when mothers stayed at home with the children. At the very same time these same Americans are strongly in favor of mothers getting off the welfare rolls. This is the big dichotomy that prevents them from grasping the importance of the relevant point. If funding is not invested in the well-being of children when they are young and vulnerable, society will pay for it's short-sightedness by having to build more prisons and distributing more welfare checks to citizens who are socially and intellectually misfit and financially dependent.

There is a ground swell moving in the direction of reform, however. There are some political leaders who are devoted to addressing the problem. The National Governors' Association (NGA) and the National Conference of State Legislators are studying the issue of helping children to get the best possible start in life. As a result of the NGA conference of October 97, state expenditures for early childhood education are on the rise in many states.. The First Lady is a strong advocate and spokesperson for the cause. She and President Clinton hosted a White House conference on the subject. Shortly after, President Clinton proposed that $22 billion be spent over the next five years to improve child care. Several members of Congress also jumped on the band wagon. Still, political bickering has the potential to scuttle these reforms. At the time of this writing, the continuing funding of the Head Start Program remains in limbo. Congress is hemming and hawing about various proposals to increase funding for the child care block grant. The President hoped to finance some of his day care package with income from the tobacco bill. The bill was in effect killed in its original form and it's future, even if revived in a weaker form, remains uncertain. Spending of any kind for the social welfare of the people is against the political philosophy of conservative lawmakers. Their main interest is in giving tax refunds and keeping spending to a minimum. Unlike their French counterparts, they do not see the value of providing quality child care to the future citizens of the United States.

In addition to funding, another problem that stands in the way of high quality child care is the lack of national standards in the field. Clear and reasonable national standards are practically non-existent. For example, each state sets its own rules regarding child-to-adult ratios. The National Association for the Education of Young Children recommends a ratio of one adult for four children under the age of nine months. Yet twenty states allow higher limits, with Idaho allowing one adult for twelve infants. Thirty-six states exceed the recommended ratio of one adult for every six two year olds. The NAEYC is a non-profit organization dedicated to improving the quality of care and education provided to our nations's young children. The Association administers the National Academy of Early Childhod Programs, a voluntary, national accreditation system for high-quality early childhood programs. Being voluntary, however, it has no authority to regulate day care centers. It can only offer a voluntary model to those who choose to operate by their suggested standards. It provides resources and services to improve professional preparation and the development of early childhood educators. It also publishes a bimonthly journal called Young Children and an array of books, brochures, videotapes and posters.

The federal government is not interestd in assuming the role of enforcer of standards. Matters of child care subsidies are under the auspices of the Department of Health and Human Resources but the department only serves to distribute the federal funds to the states through the Child Care and Development Block Grant. This $3 billion a year is then filtered through state or county social service agencies, which distribute 70% the money to needy families in the form of vouchers to be used by the parents as they see fit, either at a day care center, a home-based provider or a relative or friend. Good providers can choose not to accept the vouchers. There are no restrictions by the state as to who can receive them. If the choices for the parents are limited, the children may and often do end up in substandard or unsafe environments. The remaining 30% of federal money goes directly to day care centers and for improving the quality of existing care. The only regulatory demands that the Department of Health and Human Services makes on the states are that the states must provide matching funds, they must limit assistance to families with incomes below a certain level and they must establish minimum health and safety standards for the funded programs. However, there is little follow through on enforcing quality standards by the states.

One of the best early childhood programs in existence in the United States is the Head Start Program. This program is federally funded and federally regulated. Head Start provides comprehensive educational, health and social services to low-income children three to five who might not be getting them at home. It sees to it that the children receive their vaccinations and learn about nutrition and hygiene. It works closely with parents on improving their parenting skills. Mothers and fathers are encouraged to participate in activities and are given support and assistance in every way possible. This program qualifies (at least on paper) as a Village School. It is considerd to be highly successful. Head Start was established in 1965 as a part of Lyndon Johnson's War on Poverty. It has proved successful in raising the health, academic and social level of children who otherwise might have been disadvantaged in these areas. Research tracking the lives of these children over the past thirty-five years indicates that each dollar spent on these full-service programs returns seven dollars in reduced public expenses. These savings are due to a reduction in the need for special education, reduced teen pregnancy, less drug use, and increased levels of employment as young adults.

The following is a list of Head Start Goals as presented by the Geminus Head Start XXI School in Crown Point, Indiana:

* Help the child's emotional and social development by encouraging self-confidence, self-expression, self-discipline and curiosity.

* Improve and expand the child's ability to think, reason and speak clearly.

* Help children have varied experiences, broaden their horizons, increase their ease of conversation, and improve their understanding of the world they live in.

* Give the child frequent chances to succeed—which helps to erase patterns of frustration and failure and especially the fear of failure.

* Increase the child's ability to get along with the family, and the family to understand the child's problems, strengthen family ties.

* Develop in the child and the family a responsible attitude toward society and foster feelings of belonging to a community.

* Recognize, support and value multicultural experiences.

* Improve and maintain the child's health and nutrition.

* Help both the child and the family to have confidence, self-respect and dignity.

This is as fine and worthy a list of goals as it is possible to conceive and I would gladly adopt them for my ideal Village School. Every child deserves to be part of an early childhood program that offers services based on these goals.

In 1994, the program was extended to include day care for children zero to three and called Early Head Start. Both Head Start and Early Head Start are funded by the federal government and subject to federal standards. These standards regulate adult-to-child ratios, group sizes, number of feet of indoor space per child and the nutritional content of food. Two percent of all funds go for teacher training and twenty five percent of any funding increase must go toward program improvement, according to the new 1998 upgraded regulations. However, in spite of these high standards, Head Start still has the reputation for being uneven in the quality they deliver. Each Center is inspected only once in three years. In the meantime, many serious problems can arise and fester.

Of the estimated ten million families eligible for federal aid, only 800,000 are served by Head Start. Only 1 million are receiving subsidies through the Child Care and Development Block Grant program. Many states have waiting lists into the tens of thousands, with as long as a two year wait. Even substandard care is too expensive for many families to handle alone. Child care costs average about $3,800 a year. Parents earning less than $14,400 a year spend about 25% on day care, according to a 1995 report by the Census Bureau.

For the slightly more affluent members of society, there are more choices. Some are well-to-do working professionals who can afford to hire full-time nannies. Some nannies are highly trained and have experience with caring for children. The average cost is $300-$500 a week for a live-in and $8-$12 an hour for a day worker. Parents have to pay Social Security and other taxes, and pay health insurance premiums. They often are expected to provide transportation. Parents also have the choice of hiring *au pairs.* These are college-age girls from other countries who come to the United States under an exchange program. They are paid an average of $140 a week and given room and board. They can work only up to 45 hours a week.

Most middle income parents choose to place their children in private day care centers. The quality of these run the whole gamut from excellent to mediocre to poor. Well-informed and conscientious parents will research until they find one that is of high quality at a price they can afford. The average cost is about $70-$150 a week. Recommendations are available at religious organizations and neighborhood schools. Friends who have had successful experiences are the best source. Some 8,000 American companies offer day care directly to their employees as part of an employment package. These are usually professionally administrated and well run due to their high visibility. Many working parents prefer to have their children cared for in a private home. Often it is in the home of a relative they trust. Or it may be in the home of a neighbor or friend who needs extra income. In these cases it is important that the parents know what is happening when they are away. They must be sensitive to the child's feelings toward the caregiver and be careful to form a partnership with the person who is in charge of raising their child. Whichever form of child care a parent chooses or can afford, it is important for us as a nation to establish universal standards to protect all children from overcrowed conditions, unsafe environments and unqualified personnel. Infractions must carry serious penalties. Inspections must be frequent and unannounced to be effective. Parents must be educated as to what to look for and be encouraged to report caregivers who do not operate up to the standards. .

Realistically, we cannot expect that the federal government will offer universal day care to every family free of charge anytime in the near future. It would be prohibitively costly. However, the government can do better than it has done. A compromise can be worked out in which the parents would contribute to the care of their children according to a sliding scale depending on how much they can afford by income. The government, both state and federal, can do much to improve the quality of existing day care schools by raising standards and making them universal, consistent and mandatory. They must also raise the level of salaries and other compensations so that they are on a par with all other teachers. Parents must not expect the government to do it all. They must make themselves responsible for a large share of the burden. They can make their voices heard. They ultimately must be the judges of what constitutes quality care and convey to the caregivers their expectations. They must not settle for less.

The National Association of Child Care Resource and Referrel Agencies opened its February 2000 symposium in Washington, D.C. with the following question: **Can you think of a more compelling reason to engage in policy exploration and dialogue on early learning than the following five facts?**

* The children of 2010 can expect to spend much of their early years in the care of someone other than their parents. All who care for children are the earliest teachers.

* The children of 2010 are demographically more diverse than their predecessors; in time no single racial or ethnic group will constitute the majority of the U.S. population.

* The children of 2010 require quality programs to become effective students and adults. The cost of assuring high quality, developmentally appropriate, culturally sensitive and inclusive early education experiences is high.

* The children of 2010 deserve a major share of national resources. Creative financing strategies are necessary to harness sufficient capital to ensure a strong system of quality care and education as a birthright to all American children.

And by no means least:

* At the beginning of the year 2000, we have not achieved the goal of having "every child entering school ready to learn."

Communities around the country must begin to organize and to address their future based on these facts. We the educators, parents and citizens must develop the vision and the leadership to deliver this birthright to our children. We must encourage public policies and community programs that will make it happen. We must move our nation toward investment in the lives of our children and in our own future as a nation.

References

Collins, James. ***The Day Care Dilemma.*** Time, Feb 3,1997

Cottle, Michelle. ***Who's Watching the Kids?*** The Washington Monthly, July/August 1998.

Ellsworth, Jeanne and Ames, Linda J. Critical Perspectives on Project Head Start Albany, NY: State University of New York Press,1998.

Fuerst, J.S. and Petty, Roy. ***The best use of federal funds for early childhood education. Head Start.*** Phi Delta Kappan, June 1996 v77 n 10 p 676 (3).

Schweinhart, Lawrence J. and Weikart, David P. ***Evidence That Good Early Childhood Programs Work.*** Phi Delta Kappan, Apr 1985, pp. 545-51.

CHAPTER 13 The Growth of a Profession

Ideally, the mother of an infant will stay at home with her baby for the first year of his life. She will cuddle him, talk to him, smile at him, breast feed him and create a warm bond of love with which to surround him. No substitute caregiver can replace that kind of love. In the best of all possible worlds, the mother will be the main caregiver for at least the first three years or beyond, and she will watch him grow. The next best person to fill that role might be a grandmother who has genuine love for the child and a large store of patience and wisdom. Yet, the reality is that many mothers do not have that choice. There are single mothers who must make a living. They cannot afford to stay home for a year. They may not have a grandparent to depend on. They are forced to entrust their baby's care to a stranger and hope for the best. Then, some mothers are so career oriented that they would feel stifled in an exclusively domestic role and they feel that they must pursue their professional inclinations for the sake of their own mental health. Stay-at-home mothers do not receive very high status in our materialistic culture. Women are judged by how much money they can earn and by their ability to be independent. Perhaps this is the reason that teachers of young children are held in such low regard and subsequently so underpaid. The Women's Liberation Movement has contributed to a vague discontent with the role of homemaker. Welfare mothers are being forced into the workforce, although the new statutes do make allowances during the first year of a child's life. The following is an Associated Press release dated 02/04/00:

Kids suffer when moms leave welfare for work, study says
Associated Press

Washington — When single mothers move from welfare to the workforce, their young children often suffer from poor child care that can hinder their development, researchers said Thursday.

Most of those receiving poor care spend hours watching television with little exposure to reading and often wander aimlessly with little direction from adults, according to a study that examined the impact of welfare reform on families.

"The results are terribly distressing for young children," Yale University researcher Sharon Lynn Kagan said. "We know how to deliver quality child care and early education, we know that parents are eager to find it and we know that children who benefit from it the most—children in poor families—are facing unequal access."

Researchers from Yale University and the University of California at Berkeley randomly selected 948 single mothers with young children during the second half of 1998.

The families had all recently enrolled in welfare programs, and about a third went to work during the six-month study. The researchers interviewed the mothers, visited their child care providers and studied the children's early language and social skills.

This is evidence not only that children are better off with their own mothers, but also that much of the day care that is available leaves much to be desired. It is true that in some unfortunate instances, a mother may be so emotionally immature, so concerned with her own comfort level, that she physically or mentally abuses or neglects the child, and so he may be better off in the care of another person. But, it must be someone who is qualified, not only in terms of knowledge and education, but qualified to give the right amount of tender loving care to offset the damage done by the mother. Although being with a loving mother, or father, in warm and intimate proximity for most of the day is the most beneficial for the child, he can grow in healthy ways, given good quality care by well-trained and loving caregivers and spending quality time with the parents. The caregivers must be more than baby-sitters who merely keep him warm and fed and dry. They must have the ability to form a unique relationship with the child. It is through this caring interaction that he learns about himself and his world, who to trust and what to value. These caregivers must be warm, intelligent and self-confident individuals who feel pride in themselves and fulfillment in their work.

In spite of all the knowledge that we as a society have accumulated in the past and in spite of our verbal committment to the principles of quality care, the truth is that day care workers in these United States are not treated as first-class citizens. Typically, the younger the child, the lesser the value placed on the teacher. We seem to appreciate the importance of developing and maintaining a well-trained quality staff of elementary school teachers. They are provided with health insurance, vacation pay and pension plans in addition to a living wage. They are also given respect and status in their positions. When it comes to day care teachers, however, no such value is placed on them. The general feeling is that any idiot can take care of an infant or toddler and any warm body will do. The District of Columbia and 39 other states do not require home-based caregivers to have any prior training and 32 states don't even require training for teachers in day care centers. No matter how much training a teacher does have, the pay is so poor as to be pitiful. A 1988 study by the Center for the Child Care Work Force concluded that "child care teaching staff earned less than half as much as comparably educated women and less than one-third as much as comparably educated men in the civilian labor force." In 1985, California launched a welfare-to-work program called GAIN. Welfare recipients in the program were discouraged from considering child care as a career choice because the low pay would not lead them out of poverty. An updated study in 1997 showed that wages had remained essentially unchanged since the 1988 study. By contrast, the French, who are "contributing to the future citizens of France," pay their day care teachers a salary comparable to elementary school teachers.

The turnover of day care staff in our country is about 30% to 40% annually as a result of these poor conditions, according to a National Child-Care Staffing Study. Those caregivers and teachers who choose the profession because of a genuine love of young children are too frequently lured into greener pastures of employment, since they can earn more bagging groceries or being a parking attendant. Young children need consistency from their day care environment. The most important factor in the success of their experience is the steady, close relationship they form with their caregivers. When these relationships are disrupted repeatedly, these little ones suffer an extreme loss of security and a loss of confidence in their surroundings. This is the heart of the matter for early childhood education. Good professionally planned and administered preschools and child care facilities, with well-trained and qualified teachers who are adequately compensated for their work, who are appreciated and respected as professionals are the only solution to this crisis. For intelligent and effective college students to be attracted to the field of early childhood education there must be hope of job satisfaction for the future and for professional development. The attitude that early childhood education is only a glorified kind of baby-sitting must be changed. It must be viewed as the honored profession that it deserves to be.

What other profession carries as much responsibility for the lives of children? Would we turn our children over to a pediatrician who was not adequately trained? Would we allow him to prescribe medications and perform surgery if we did not have the security of knowing that he was a state certified, trained professional with our children's best interest at heart? Wouldn't we want to see his credentials? Would we pay him one third less than other physicians because his patients happen to be very young? Caring for the minds and personalities and spirits of young children is surely as important a job as caring for their bodies. Early childhood teaching deserves to be on a professional par with pediatrics. There can be no compromise if we have our childrens' best interests at heart. They are our future citizens and our dearly beloved.

In order to raise the profession to this desired level we must adhere to a conceptual framework for early childhood professional development. This transformation must necessarily occur in gradual steps to take it from where it now stands to the highest level. The unqualified must become qualified or be gone. Currently, many early childhood practioners have not completed formal preparation programs. They gain training through a hit-and-miss approach that often reflects their state's child licensing requirements or the lack of training opportunities in their area. To be a true professional, a teacher of high caliber must have a broad, liberal education. She or he must study child development, educational history and philosophy, the behavioral sciences, early childhood curriculum and elementary curriculum. Effective professional development must also involve linking theory and practice much as the training in the field of medicine links theory and practice. The training for both fields would be meaningless if it was limited to only book learning. Trainees must be under the tutelage of experienced practitioners and learn strategies that are effective in actual situations. They can apply what they are learning immediately with a hands-on approach and receive immediate feedback They can reflect on what is happening and integate its meaning into their own professional repetoire. It is equally important to establish a broad foundation of theoretical knowledge and to develop a base of skills and strategies from practical experiences. This principle ensures both legitimacy and credibility in the profession. It gives the practitioner a positive self-esteem and a strong philosophical structure on which to rely with assurance. All early childhood professionals need to continually add to their skills and knowledge. Professional development is an on-going process.

Becoming qualified for this level of professional integrity requires time and committment. There would be little incentive for pursuing such a career unless increased qualifications bring rewards of adequate compensation. But, before such a goal can be reached, early childhood programs would need additional resources. Families alone could not bear the burden of these higher costs. The National Associated for the Education of Young Childen (NAEYC) is committed to strategies that would distribute these costs more equitably among all sectors of society. All of society, and the nation as a whole, benefits from the provision of high quality education to young children. Early childhood professionals and parents have borne a disproportionate share of the burden. It is time that this essential service be shared by all sectors of our society, including state and federal governments and the business community.

Early childhood professionals work in a variety of settings: child care centers, public and private pre-school programs, public school kindergartens, Head Start and Early Head Start, after-school programs, and family child care, in which their responsibilities are similar. Regardless of the setting of their job, if they have comparable qualifications, experience and responsibilities, they should receive comparable compensation for their work. Removing the disparity in pay within various early childhood settings is a worthy goal. However, it is not enough, since the profession as a whole is so undervalued to begin with. Salary scales and benefits must be compared to those in other professional groups. Reviews should be conducted within the community and within the early childhood program's larger organizational structure to determine what the standard should be for comparable professionals with the same education, experience and responsibility. For example, early childhood teachers might be compared to social workers, counselors, nurses, elementary school teachers and secondary school teachers. Their services are equally valuable and they should be compensated accordingly. Salaries should not be differentiated on the basis of the ages of the children served. The inclusion of a benefits package, (sick leave, vacation time, health insurance and retirement fund) should be provided as well. If the employee feels valued in this way, he or she will have an incentive to remain on the job, will be able to concentrate on teaching and will be more likely to convey positive feelings toward the children. Family child care providers, who are self-employed, would also have a standard on which to base their fees for providing high quality service.

All students of early childhood education and practitioners should plan and design their own professional development program. There are six levels of preparation for which standards have been established nationally by the **National Association for the Education of Young Children** (the AMA of the early childhood profession.) The following table illustrates the preparation necessary to achieve each professional level according to guidelines from the NAEYC:

Early Childhood Professional Level I

Individuals who are employed in an early childhood professional role working under supervision or with support and participating in training designed to lead to the assessment of individual competencies or acquisition of a degree. (Student Teachers)

Early Childhood Professional Level II

II. A. Successful completion of the CDA Professional Preparation Program OR completion of a systematic comprehensive training program that prepares an individual to successfully acquire the CDA Credential through direct assessment. (CDA: Child Development Association.)

II. B. Successful completion of a one-year early childhood certificate program.

Early Childhood Professional Level III

Successful completion of an associate degree from a program conforming to NAEYC guidelines; OR Successful completion of an associate degree in a related field, plus 30 units of professional studies in early childhood development/education including 300 hours of supervised teaching experience in an early childhood program; OR successful demonstation of the knowledge, performance, and dispositions expected as outcomes of an associate degree program conforming to NAEYC guidelines. (Assistant Teacher)

Early Childhood Professional Level IV

Successful completion of a baccalaureate degree from a program conforming to NAEYC guidelines; OR State certificate meeting NAEYC guidelines; OR Successful completion of a baccalaureate degree in another field with more than 30 professional units in early childhood development/education including 300 hurs of supervised teaching experience, including 150 hours each for two of the following three age groups: infants and toddlers, 3-to-5-year olds, or the primary grades; OR Successful demonstration of the knowledge, performance, and dispositions expected as outcomes of a baccalaureate degree program conforming to NAEYC guidelines. (Head Teacher)

Early Childhood Professional Level V

Successful completion of a master's degree program that conforms to NAEYC guidelines; OR Successful demonstration of the knowledge, performance, and dispositions expected as outcomes of a master's degree program conforming to NAEYC guidelines.

Early Childhood Professional Level VI

Successful completion of a Ph.D or Ed.D. in a program conforming to NAEYC guidelines; OR

Successful demonstration of the knowledge, performance, and dispositions expected as outcomes of a doctoral degree program conforming to NAEYC guidelines.

Underlying the achievement of these professional levels, of course, is the factor of the personality of the individual teacher and his or her committment to the welfare of children. Early childhood teaching is not only a science but an art as well. It requires a certain quality of personality. There are many people who have fine qualities who do not have a degree in early childhood education but who have good instincts concerning children. This is perhaps more important than a degree. However, it would be difficult to assess and monitor their qualifications.

The parents themselves would have to judge whether they were reliable and capable. If I were a parent who must entrust her precious child to another, I would not settle for anyone who did not have these qualities: patience, emotional stability, flexibility, empathy for and a belief in people, a thoughtful mind, and a warm and nurturing nature. She or he would also know how to communicate with children and understand how they learn and how to provide experiences for them that would enhance their intellectual, physical and personal growth. She would understand the difference between discipline and punishment and be able to teach discipline consistently and lovingly. She would understand that children grow at their own rate and, like seeds, will grow into readiness according to their own biological clock.

I have a dream— that all early childhood teaching will take place in the Village Schools of tomorrow, where *all* young children will be given an equal opportunity to grow to their most promising potential. Parents and teachers will be partners in nurturing and teaching. Parent centers will be an integral part of each school where parents will be able to learn about their children and improve their parenting skills with the help of teachers, counselors, and administrators, and through seminars, discussions and guest speakers. They will be introduced to literature and articles on the subject of parenting. They will have an opportunity to meet other parents and share their experiences in the relaxed atmosphere of the "village." Village Schools will have a blueprint based on the best of programs that are available now and those yet to be born. These programs will follow guidelines that are founded on a heart-felt philosophy of education. The preservation of human dignity will take the highest priority. Teaching self-confidence, self-respect, independence, self-control, self-mastery and respect for others will be the primary goals. Teachers of young children will be highly respected members of the community and compensated adequately for their contribution in helping to shape the minds and hearts of our future citizens. They will greet each day with pleasure and end each day with satisfaction and with pride in their hearts.

References

Association of Teacher Educators (ATE) and National Association for the Education of Young Children (NAEYC) Early Childhood Teacher Certification. *Young Children*, 47, (1), 1991, 16-21.

Bloom, P.J. Full cost of quality report. But I'm worth more than that!: Addressing employee concerns about compensation. *Young Children,* 48 (3) 1993, 65-68.

Bredekamp, S. *Regulating child care quality: Evidence from NAEYC's accredation system.* Washington, D.C.: NAEYC, 1989.

Epstein, A.S. *Training for quality: Improving early childhood programs through systematicv inservice training.* Monographs of the High/Scope Educational Research Foundation, Number Nine. Ypsilanti, MI: High/Scope Educational research Foundation, 1993.

Pear, Robnert. *Child Care Initiative Planned.* New York Times, Dec 14, 1997.

Schultz, Tom and Lopez, M. Elena. *Early childhood reform: local innovations on a flawed policy system.* Phi Delta Kappan, Sept 1995 v 77 nl p 60 (4).

Wheelock College. *Taking the Lead: Investing in Early Childhood Leadership for the 21st Century.* Boston, Mass. The Center for Career Development in Early Care and Education, 2000.

Bibliography

Association of Teacher Educators (ATE) and National Association for the Education of Young Children (NAEYC) Early Childhood Teacher Certification. *Young Children,* 47 (1), 1991, 16-21.

Bloom, P.J. Full cost of quality report. "But I'm worth more than that!: Addressing employee concerns about compensation. *Young Children,* 48 (3) 1993, 65-68.

Bredekamp, S. *Regulating child care quality: Evidence from NAEYC's accredation system.* Washington, D.C.: NAEYC, 1989.

Cohen, Dorothy H. The Learning Child. New York: Vintage Books: Random House, 1973.

Collins, James. *The Day Care Dilemma*. Time, Feb 3, 1997.

Cottle, Michelle. *Who's Watching the Kids?* The Washington Monthly, July/August 1998.

Chukovsky, Kornei. From Two to Five. University of California Press, 1968.

Dewey, John. Democracy and Education. New York: Macmillan Company, 1916.

Dewey, John. School and Society. Chicago: University of Chicago Press, 1900.

Dewey, John and Dewey, Evelyn. Schools of Tomorrow. New York: E.P. Dutton & Co., Inc., 1915.

Ellsworth, Jeanne and Ames, Lynda J. Critical Perspectives on Project Head Start Albany, NY: State University of New York Press, 1998.

.Epstein, A.S. *Training for quality: Improving early childhood programs through systematic inservice training.* Monographs of the High/Scope Educational Research Foundation, Number Nine. Ypsilanti, MI: High/ScopeEducational Research Foundation, 1993.

Feldman, W.T. The Philosophy of John Dewey. Washington, D.C.: The Johns Hopkins Press, 1934.

Fisher, Dorothy Canfield. Montessori for Parents. Cambridge, Mass.: Robert Bentley, Inc., 1965.

Fraiberg, Selma. The Magic Years. New York: Charles Scribner's Sons, 1959.

Froebel, Friedrich. The Education of Man. New York: D. Appleton & Company, 1887.

Fuerst, J.S. and Petty, Roy. *The best use of federal funds for early chilhood education. Head Start* Phi Delta Kappan, June 1996 v77 n 10 p 676 (3).

Gandini, L. *The Hundred Languages of Children: The Reggio Emilia Approach to Early Childhood Education.* Norwood, NJ: Ablex ED 355 034, 1993.

Havinghurst, Robert J. and Neugarten, Bernice L. Society and Education. Boston: Allyn & Bacon, Inc., 1962.

Hendel, Charles W. John Dewey and the Experimental Spirit in Philosophy. New York: The Liberal Arts Press, 1959.

Homan, William E. *Discipline means "to teach."* The New York Times Magazine, March 16, 1969.

Ilg, Frances L.; Ames, Louise Bates. Child Behavior. New York: Dell Publishing Company, Inc., 1955.

Katz, L.G. and Cesarone, B. ***Reflectionson the Reggio Emilia Approach.*** Urbana, IL: ERIC Clearinghouse on Elementary and Early Childhood Education. ED 375 986, 1994.

Kocher, Marjorie B. The Montessori Manual of Cultural Subjects. Minneapolis: Denison & Company, Inc., 1923.

Landeck, Beatrice. Songs to Grow On. New York: Edward B. Marks Music Corp-Wm. Sloan Associates, 1950.

Lane, Howard; Beauchamp, Mary. Understanding Human Behavior. Englewood Cliffs, NJ: Prentice Hall, Inc., 1959.

Law, Norma; Moffitt, Mary; Moore, Elenora; Overfield, Ruth; Starks, Esther. Basic Propositions for Early Childhood Education. Washington, D.C. Association for Childhood Education International, 1966.

Lilly, Irene M. Friedrich Froebel. Cambridge, Mass.: Cambridge University Press, 1967.

Montessori, Maria. The Montessori Method. Cambridge, Mass.: Robert Bentley, Inc., 1912.

Montessori, Maria. Dr. Montessori's Own Handbook. New York: Schocken Books, 1914.

Moustakos, Clark. The Authentic Teacher: Sensitivity and Awareness in the Classroom. Cambridge Mass.: Howard A. Doyle Publishing Company, 1966.

Nash, J. Madeleine. ***Fertile Minds.*** Time, Feb 3, 1997

Pear, Robert. ***Child Care Initiative Planned***, New York Times, Dec 14, 1997.

Rogers, Carl. Freedom to Learn. Columbus, Ohio: Charles E. Merrill Publishing Company, 1969.

Schultz, Tom; Lopez, M. Elena. *Early childhood reform: local innovations in a flawed policy system.* Phi Delta Kappan, Sept 1995 v77 nl p60 (4).

Schweinhart, Lawrence J. and Weikart, David P. *Evidence That Good Early Childhood Programs Work.* Phi Delta Kappan, Apr 1985, pp. 545-51.

Thompson, George G. Child Psychology. Boston, Mass.: Houghton Mifflin Company, 1962.

Wheelock College. Boston, Mass. The Center for Career Development in Early Care and Education. *Taking the Lead: Investing in Early Childhood Leadership for the 21st Century,* 2000.

ABOUT THE AUTHOR

Georgia Palmer was born and raised in New York City where she received her BA at Hunter College and her MSed from Bank Street College of Education. She taught pre-school and kindergarten for 12 years in a private school setting prior to moving to Phoenix, Arizona. Although early childhood education has always been her first love, she found that she could not make a living in the field at a time when it became necessary to support herself. She therefore attended Arizona State University and became certified to teach special education and received a master's degree in guidance counseling. She worked for the Phoenix Union High School District for 18 years, 10 as a special education teacher, and 8 as a guidance counselor. Now retired, her interest in the education of young children is still a flame. Sadly, early childhood teachers are still not on a level with other teachers when it comes to salary, fringe benefits and respect or status. She strives to raise the profession to a level at which competent teachers who love to work with the youngest children will be able to afford to do so. She has two grown daughters and one grandson and now lives in Phoenix with her husband, Joe, and her dog, Sparky.

www.ingramcontent.com/pod-product-compliance
Ingram Content Group UK Ltd.
Pitfield, Milton Keynes, MK11 3LW, UK
UKHW041937190726
13854UKWH00004B/1635